Cracking the Dream Code

A Biblical and Practical Approach to Dream Interpretation

Jumoke Ayo-Ajayi

Copyright © 2020 by Jumoke Ayo-Ajayi
All rights reserved
JumokeA.com
CrackingTheDreamCode.com

ISBN 979-8-6873955-4-0

This book or parts thereof may not be reproduced in any form, stored in any retrieval system, or transmitted in any form by any means—electronic, mechanical, photocopy, recording, or otherwise—without prior written permission of the publisher, except as provided by United States of America copyright law.

Unless otherwise stated, all scriptures are taken from *The Holy Bible, New International Version ®*, NIV® Copyright © 1973, 1978, 1984, 2011 by Biblica, Inc.® Used by permission. All rights reserved worldwide.

Cover Design by Rebecca Justilien
Edited by Rebecca Justilien

Dedication

This book is dedicated to all the dreamers who desire to grow in dream interpretation.

Table of Contents

Acknowledgments xxiv
Preface xxvi
Introduction 1
Part One | All About the Dream Code 7
What Are Dreams? 9
Who Gets Meaningful Dreams? 10
Why Do We Get Dreams? 12
What is Dream Interpretation? 14
What is Biblical Interpretation? 14
Where Do Dreams Come From? 21
    Understanding the Spiritual Realm 21
    The Source of Dreams 23
    Dreams from God 23
    Dreams from Demons 47
    Dreams from Ourselves 68
    External Dreams 70
    Lucid Dreaming 70
Preparing to Dream 73
    Sleep Hygiene 75
    How to Record Dreams 79
    Remembering Dreams 80
Part Two | How to Crack the Dream Code 83

The Methodology 87
Different Levels of Dreams 89
Different Types of Dreamers 93
How God Speaks to You 96
Understanding Symbolism 100
Perfectionism vs Grace 108
Maybe Faith 109
The Holy Spirit 110
Folding (Decoding Symbols) 112
Organizing (Interpretation) 120
Putting Away (Application) 125
Troubleshooting 134
Part Three | The Dream Code 139
Characters 142
A Character Representing Yourself 142
A Character Representing God 143
Characters Representing Angels 147
Characters Representing Demons 148
Characters Representing Symbols 151
Common Experiences 162
Running away/getting chased 162
Falling 164
Laughing 165
Fighting 166
Waiting in Line 167
Flying 168

Being Late 169
Being Lost 171
Nakedness 172
Pregnancy, Birth & Babies 172
Romantic Encounters 174
Death 188
Part Four | Let's Get Crackin'! 193
Examples 196
Conclusion 229
Appendix 235
Dream Dictionary 237
Setting 240
Houses/Rooms & Their Content 242
Places 251
Nature 257
Colors 262
Numbers 266
Finances 274
Transportation 277
Sports 284
Human Anatomy 285
Clothes 291
Food & Drink 296
Animals 300
Communication 304
Resources 307

Acknowledgments

I would like to acknowledge everyone who has contributed to this work.

I would first like to thank my Lord and Savior, Jesus Christ, through whom all things are possible. Without You, I don't know where I'd be.

I would like to thank my loving parents for supporting me through my whole journey and being a source of encouragement in everything I put my mind to. This book would not be possible without you two.

I would like to thank my close friends for standing by my side since college. Thank you Esi, Dammy, Sope, Elizabeth, Rebecca, and Chino for your prayers and being my community and covenant friends. Special shout out to Soul Sistas as well.

I would finally like to thank every viewer, subscriber, and mentee who has crossed paths with me. Without your presence, I would have never discovered my purpose. Thank you for pushing me into my callings.

Preface

Cracking the Dream Code seeks to help dreamers understand and interpret their dreams in a biblical and practical way. This book is for those who dream, cannot make sense of their dreams, but have an understanding that dreams carry some significance.

This book is also for the dreamer who can make some sense of their dream but would like to grow in biblical interpretation and gain a practical approach in this area.

Introduction

You wake up in a panic. You just had a vivid dream, but you have no idea what it means. Although it seemed completely random, the fact that you could remember every detail and theme gives you the push to investigate. For some reason, something within you tells you to take this seriously. You may pray and ask God for clarity, or you may jump right to Google. You may google some details in your dream to see if anything resonates, or you may be like me and avoid Google altogether because you don't trust certain sources. Regardless, you keep pondering on this dream to the point that you end up with more questions than answers. You may also have so many dreams to count that at this point, you've given up entirely on understanding the meaning of your dreams.

This was me. Although I've had dreams my whole life, my gift of dreaming didn't amplify until I got saved. Since I got saved in 2014, I have dreamt literally almost every. Single. Night. Now I didn't mind being entertained by these mind movies, but what in the world did they mean?! Unless a dream was literal, I disregarded them into the abyss of my Note App, and I would get so frustrated and ask God to just speak to me plainly. Most of my dreams seemed like straight gibberish, and sometimes I would feel dumb for not understanding it. To add insult to injury, I would read the Bible and get convicted through the lives of Joseph and Daniel, who had a gift of interpreting dreams.

So, this went on for a couple of years. Meanwhile, I continued to serve the Lord and others through my YouTube platform, and one day, a viewer commented on a natural hair video and told me to check out a minister's YouTube channel. Mind you, I had faith videos, and this comment seemed unrelated. Nevertheless, I checked out the page, and it was Kevin Ewing's channel who just so happened to have a dream ministry. I was ecstatic! I was truly amazed by how God answered my prayer to understand dreams.

For the next few months, I completely submerged myself into the world of dream interpretation through Kevin Ewing. I listened to every video he had on this topic, and I even went to his blog to learn more. Since his videos were a bit long-winded, I thought it would be wise to create a personal dream journal through the entries of his blog. I probably combed through a hundred of his blog posts, and I jotted down notes and symbols from each. I figured one day all his information wouldn't be free, so I took the opportunity.

Once I had my dream journal, I thought I was fully equipped to dive headfirst into the area of dream interpretation. I began using the symbols provided as a guideline to interpreting my dreams and others' dreams. I even made my first dream interpretation YouTube video based on the symbols that I had acquired. But then... The more and more I interpreted dreams, I began to realize some serious issues.

For one, I didn't have an exhaustive list of dream symbols. When I would interpret my or others' dreams, I would freak out when I got to a symbol that I did not understand or was exposed to. *What in the world does Chick-Fil-A mean in a dream?!*

The next issue I noticed was the one-sidedness of symbols. From my dream journal, the majority of symbols were negative or demonic, resulting in interpretations that were mostly negative or demonic. Now don't get me wrong. Many people, especially Christians, are utterly ignorant of the plans of the enemy, the kingdom of darkness, witchcraft, and spiritual warfare. I believe that believers should be equipped in this way, but I also think that there should be a balance. In any regard, I became heavily reliant on my dream journal to help me to interpret dreams, and I was not growing in my gift of interpretation. I was ill-equipped to discern the different sources of dreams as well as the context of a symbol.

The last issue I saw was the lack of beginner-friendly dream interpretation teaching. It wasn't until a year after my initial exposure to dream interpretation that I began to branch out to other dream ministries. Although they offered more well-rounded symbol dictionaries, their approach to interpreting dreams was not practical. I noticed that most dream interpretation instructors would either approach interpretation through a more symbolic side (as in just interpreting dreams through a symbol library) or through a more prophetic side (as in only relying on the Holy Spirit and the gifts of the Spirit). For someone new to dream interpretation, these systems are not practical in and of themselves. Every symbol will not be in a dictionary, and not everyone can teach others to tap into the prophetic realm.

These experiences have led me to not only figure out a better way to interpret dreams, but I discovered methods to *teach* others how to do it. Through my gift of teaching, I have been able to equip many others to interpret their dreams devoid of being dependent on dream dictionaries. Many people don't realize that *they* are the best person to interpret their dreams because dreams are highly subjective and self-centered. Through my experience of interpreting countless dreams, I discovered that 90% of dreams are about you. Yep. It's wild, huh? You would think that with all the randomness and different characters that it would be a small percentage, but no.

Now with that knowledge, it's a shame the majority of our dreams are discarded as some would call "pizza dreams." Just a random junk of nothingness that was probably a result of something we've eaten. Do you want to know another fun fact? Through my experience, I've been able to give meaning to almost all the dreams that come my way. Whether my own dreams or others. You may or may not be impressed, but this is not the result of only a special anointing. I believe dream interpretation is simply a language that any believer can learn and grow through practice. It grieves me to know that everyone has dreams, but not many understand them! Imagine, a whole lifetime goes by without clarity of one's dreams. Someone could be missing out on so many God messages without even realizing it! Dreams communicating business plans, creative solutions to life problems, foretelling of what's to come, warnings, insight, and the list goes on.

Through this book, I hope to equip you, the reader, with the tools you need to begin or to grow in your understanding of dream interpretation. I'll walk you step-by-step into the mind of a master dream interpreter. You'll discover tips and tricks to overcome most hurdles and excel in this area. Finally, you will be able to understand what God is trying to communicate to you and crack the dream code.

Part One | All About the Dream Code

What Are Dreams?

So, what in the world are dreams?! Are they just a bunch of mumbo jumbo, or do they signify something deeper? According to the Internet, "A dream is a succession of images, ideas, emotions, and sensations that usually occur involuntarily in the mind during certain stages of sleep." Other sources say that dreams are basically stories our mind makes up while we sleep. That sounds pretty basic, and it seems like something that *just* happens, but are dreams normal? It seems that most people have just accepted dreams because it happens without much of our control, but are dreams actually *good*? Also, *who* can get significant dreams? Is this phenomenon strictly reserved for believers or can *anyone* receive meaningful dreams?

To start, the Holy Bible validates dreams and reveals that they are, indeed, meaningful, and it is a way that God communicates to us. The Scriptures say, *In the last days, God says, I will pour out my Spirit on all people. Your sons and daughters will prophesy, your young men will see visions, your old men will dream dreams (Acts 2:17 NIV).* Friends, these are truly the last days as we see signs of the end times all around us, and God is communicating to people through dreams like never before. If God uses dreams as a medium to speak to us, then how much more reverence should we give them!

Who Gets Meaningful Dreams?

Furthermore, meaningful dreams are not "just a Christian thing." It may seem like that sometimes because we as Christians may unknowingly project that God only cares and talks to Christians. *Y'all... If that ain't further from the truth!* Listen. It *is* true that God communicates and cares for believers differently, but His love is for the whole world. The Bible says that God SO loved the WORLD that He gave His only begotten Son that whoever believes in Him shall not perish but have eternal life (John 3:16). God wanted reconciliation with His children, so He sent His Son Jesus Christ to die for our sins. Jesus didn't die and resurrect *just* for morally good people, but He died for everyone including you and me.

So, you may be asking, *Okay God wants to speak to everyone but is there proof of that?* I'm glad you asked (and even if you didn't, I'm still going to tell you anyway)! There are some examples in the Bible of God using dreams to speak to believers and unbelievers which we will explore.

The first example is of Joseph, son of Jacob, in the Old Testament. He is a very famous biblical dreamer, and we will discuss some of his techniques and lessons while we continue on with this book. Joseph had future dreams by God that came to pass later on in his life. He also interpreted the dream God had given Pharaoh who was an unbeliever.

Another example of a well-known dreamer was Daniel. Daniel had a prophetic dream (a dream that predicts the future) and was able to discover the interpretation of that dream. Daniel was also able to interpret King Nebuchadnezzar's dream who, again, was an unbeliever.

Other examples of dreamers in the bible include Jacob, King Abimelech, Solomon, Joseph (Jesus's earthly father), the wise men, Pilate's wife, and John. As we can see, God uses dreams to connect with different types of people at different points in time.

Dreams or Visions?

So, what's the difference between a dream and a vision? In basic terms, you have dreams when you sleep, and you have visions while you're awake. Typically, people who have a gift of seeing into the spiritual realm (i.e. seeing angels, demons, and other supernatural phenomena), or seers, are more prone to having visions. We'll discuss more about seeing as a way God speaks to us in a later section.

Why Do We Get Dreams?

So, we've discussed what dreams are, but why do we get them in the first place? Why can't we just close our eyes, sleep, and wake up? Well, we receive dreams for a few reasons which include: for God to speak to us, so we can see the strategies of the enemy in our lives, and so we can see what's going on in our soul. Too many people throw away dreams because they seem completely random, but there are so many messages packed into dreams that we should take them seriously.

To start, it's crucial to understand God's heart towards you as His son or daughter. Throughout our lives, God continues to pursue us through His love, and He wants to reconnect with us in a way we can understand. Some people hate the thought of receiving messages from God through their dreams because they truly don't get what He is trying to say. I just want to tell you that it is not His nature to bring confusion, and He indeed wants you to hear Him. God wants to have an intimate relationship with you that is devoid of mundane rituals, so sometimes He speaks through dreams to shake things up.

If we think about it, it makes sense that God would want to speak to us through dreams because let's be honest—we are a busy people. Sometimes we are so caught up with the hustle and bustle of our everyday life that we miss God completely, and when we are sleeping and at rest, it's the perfect time for God to download revelation to us. Not even that, but when we receive a dream that we don't understand, it pushes us to seek Him for understanding.

Moreover, we have an unforeseen enemy that is trying to divert us away from the will of God. Have you ever had a terrifying dream or a dream that felt off? It could have been a demonic dream which we will discuss more in-depth later. You may be wondering the purpose of these types of dreams because they seem like a nuisance if anything. Well, these dreams may give you a clue of the plan of the enemy in your life (we will discuss how in a later section), which you can then intersect the attack or receive clarity about why things are perspiring in your life. Getting dreams from the enemy is no joke! These dreams are nothing to play with, but Hosea 2:6 says that people are destroyed for a lack of knowledge. We must take the knowledge given to us through our dreams and fight back!

Lastly, dreams can give us an understanding of what's going on with ourselves. Sometimes the things we've experienced saw or felt can be rehashed through a dream. In a way, these types of dreams are just our minds processing what we are currently going through or what we previously went through. As we will soon learn, these dreams are not necessarily bad and can still hold key information that we were probably unaware of when we were awake.

What is Dream Interpretation?

At this point, you may be thinking, *Okay Jumoke. All of this sounds great, and I now understand that dreams are important, but why don't more people know how to interpret dreams? If the reasons you've mentioned are true, then why is the meaning of dreams difficult to grasp?* I hear you, and these are all very good conjectures to make. Since dreams are not a new phenomenon, people have been trying to make sense of their dreams for the longest. First, we have to understand there are two main ways to approach dream interpretation: biblical and unbiblical. To be successful in dream interpretation, we have to uncover the difference between the two and realize the importance of biblical dream interpretation to crack the dream code.

What is Biblical Interpretation?

If you go far enough down the rabbit hole of research about dream interpretation, you will begin to notice that many people, Christian, and non-Christian alike, have attempted to crack the dream code. To an unassuming person, any approach to dream interpretation is valid because dreams are simply a puzzle, but this is incorrect. Remember earlier when we discussed why we get dreams, and I mentioned a big reason is that God wants to speak to us? God wants to speak to us, BUT only the *Spirit* of God can interpret the *mind* of God. The Bible says, "No one can know a person's thoughts except that person's own spirit, and no one can know God's thoughts except God's own Spirit (1 Cor 2:11 NLT)." Friends, God speaks to EVERYONE through the medium of dreams, including unbelievers, BUT only a born-again believer can interpret dreams from God because of the Holy Spirit that dwells in them.

This very reason is why many who have sought understanding about their dreams sometimes become confused after gleaning information from an unbeliever. The dreamer, at most, may be able to pick up some revelation, but the full revelation of what God was trying to communicate will be lost.

Moreover, there will be some unbelievers that claim to know the answers dream hold, but friends, this is a false claim. In the word of God, many unbelievers were able to mimic miracles, signs, and wonders, but they were operating from a false source. It legitimately takes godly discernment to weed out true dream interpretation from what *seems* true.

All in all, we cannot approach dream interpretation without a biblical stance because those who do not *know* God cannot share the *mind* of God. God reveals Himself to us through the Holy Bible so if we want a solid foundation in this area, we must become and remain students of the Word while growing in intimacy with the Holy Spirit.

Literal Dreams vs Symbolic Dreams

So, when it comes to dream interpretation, there is a major key to grasp! Write this down somewhere and carry it with you wherever you go (kidding but am I really?)! The major key to dream interpretation is to understand that they fall into two categories: literal and symbolic.

Literal dreams are literally that (no pun intended). They are to the point, and what you see is what you get. There are no symbols involved, and these dreams are usually short. An example of a literal dream would be when a messenger angel came to Joseph in a dream and told him to take Mary as his wife (Matthew 1:18-25). Although it's not uncommon to have literal dreams from time to time, (spoiler alert!) the majority of dreams are symbolic. When we receive a dream, we should never rush to the assumption that it's literal, especially if there are parts that are seemingly random or wouldn't happen in real life. You should still seek to understand the mystery of dreams and what the dream is trying to convey. This is what dream interpretation is all about!

I believe the main reason people don't take their dreams seriously is that dreams are usually not straightforward. As humans, when we encounter things we don't understand, we rationalize them away. How many times have you had a bizarre dream, and instead of pressing into it, you rationalized that it must've been something you ate, saw, experienced, or dreams are just weird? Yeah. Most of us. I know it's the natural thing to do, but it is irresponsible.

What if that random dream was a God dream? If God is the One who spoke the whole universe into existence, then who are we to let His words fall to the ground? We must take the things of God seriously and steward over our gift of dreaming.

Moreover, the language of God is symbols and parables. Did you know that almost a *third* of the whole Bible is poetry? Well, God is a masterful Poet and Creator, and He uses imagery and symbolism to convey profound messages. How many times have you listened to a lecture or a sermon, and for some reason you only vividly remember the anecdotes or stories within the message? Probably a lot of us! God knows this very well which is a reason why He chooses to use symbols, parables, and poetry. The imagery of a message sticks to us a lot longer than simple words ever could.

If you are sitting there wondering why God can't just speak to you plainly is because it is the glory of God to conceal a matter, but it is up to us to seek it out (Prov 25:2). God wants you to seek Him for answers and draw close to Him. Yes, He could always talk to you plainly, but let's be honest; that may be a little terrifying (Ex 20:19). Also, God speaks to us very clearly through His Word, but many of us still are not acutely aware of how He communicates to us in our individual lives.

If you're *still* wondering why it's God's preference to communicate through symbolism, and the Bible gives us an explanation. When Jesus walked the earth, He was known for speaking in parables, which is an allegorical story filled with symbols to explain a spiritual concept. One day, His disciples questioned Him about His use of parables, and in Matthew 13:10-16 He goes on to explain His reasoning. We learned that God speaks in riddles to soften our hearts, to test our responsiveness to the Word, and to express His mercy.

Let's start with our hearts. It's interesting that Jesus gave an explanation of speaking in parables within giving a parable and its explanation (Matt 13:1-23). Jesus gave a parable about the different types of hearts people have and how they each respond differently to God's Word.

For some, the Word has no bearing in their hearts because they didn't understand it to begin with, and their hearts were hardened. Satan snatched the Word from their hearts, so they were never able to bear fruit. Furthermore, some people hear the Word and receive it immediately with joy, but it's short-lived due to trials and testing. These are the people who are enthusiastic about the faith at first, but when they come under persecution and tribulation, their lack of depth causes them to fall away. Still, some people's response to hearing the Word is to grow for a while, but they end up being unfruitful because they have other worldly things competing with their spiritual growth. This looks like believers who are trying to grow with the Lord, but they have not fully surrendered their old lives and ways unto Him. Lastly, there are those who receive the Word and produce fruit in their lives because they have a softened heart.

We have to understand that there is nothing wrong with God's Word; there's an issue with our hearts. Yeah, I get that your dreams and visions may seem odd, but is your heart softened to receive understanding? Listen to me very carefully—*There's NOTHING wrong with your dreams!* No, all your dreams are not a bunch of junk, and no, you're not the only one with weird dreams. In order to crack the dream code, we must gain a healthy reverence to symbols that show up in our dreams as they could be a way that God is trying to get His Word to us. We must always have a softened and humbled heart towards the different ways God speaks to us.

Next, let's discuss responsiveness to the Word of God. Remember earlier when I said that it is the glory of God to conceal a matter, but it is up to us to seek it out (Prov 25:2)? Well, God purposefully conceals the meaning of things to coax us to dig deeper. Think about it. If you had a treasure chest full of valuables, you would not just give it away for free. You may dig a hole in an inconspicuous place and bury it, or at least set up a contest for people to work for it! The point is, no one gives away extremely valuable things for free; usually, the person who receives it is the person who had a *high desire* for it. Likewise, symbols are used to place the responsibility on the hearer or dreamer to discover the deeper meaning.

Lastly, God speaks in riddles because that is, in fact, His mercy towards us. That may seem strange to you who are reading but hear me out. Have you ever heard the Gospel preached in a way that was not... appealing? Most people,

Christians, and non-Christians can testify that they've witnessed Christianity portrayed in a way that left a bad taste in their mouths. Most people can agree that it's not always *what* is said but *how* it is said.

Now let's go back to Jesus and the parable He gave in Matthew 13. Let's imagine that He didn't use a parable and spoke very plainly. What if He said something along the lines of—*Most of y'all are stubborn people, and you guys don't care about the Words I'm speaking. You're acting as you do, but you're too hard-headed to receive anything. So you're sitting there looking at me like you're listening, but you're actually spiritually deaf and blind!* ...Yeah. Let's keep it all the way real. If Jesus spoke like that all the time, instead of His Words bringing correction and conviction, it would have an opposite effect on people. Many people's hearts would be *further* hardened, and some would only feel condemnation. We have to know that conviction comes from God and encourages people to repent, turn from their ways, and run back to God. Condemnation, on the other hand, is from the devil, brings guilt and shame, and causes people to run and hide from God.

A learning point to take away is that part of God's character is that He is merciful and patient. God shows His mercy through parables and symbols because it encourages those with a humble heart to further seek Him for clarity, but at the same time, allows someone with a hardened heart to not fall into condemnation. What an awesome God we serve!

To recap, God uses symbols to soften our hearts, test our responsiveness to His Word, and as a way to show His mercy. Only having literal dreams seem like a fairytale to some, but is it really? As we just learned, God has specific reasons why He speaks to us using symbols, so we should not always rush to assume that only literal dreams are meaningful.

Where Do Dreams Come From?

We've learned *sooo* much about dreams already, but there's a missing piece: Where do dreams come from? In a way, dreams are our monitors to the unseen realm (aka the spiritual realm), and this is instrumental to understand as it will give us some major clues in cracking the dream code.

Understanding the Spiritual Realm

There are two main realms that exist: the physical realm and the spiritual realm (Col 1:16). The physical realm is the realm that we can feel, hear, see, taste, and smell. The spiritual realm is the unseen realm where spiritual beings such as God, angels, and demons reside (If you have ever seen the movie, *The Matrix*, then this is a very good depiction of the physical and spiritual realm).

As human beings, we coexist in the physical and the spiritual realm because we are body, soul, and spirit. However, it's important to note that we are first spirits, and our bodies are accessories to our spirits. We have a physical body that can interact with the physical realm, but our soul, on the other hand, houses our thoughts, will, and emotions. Sometimes the soul is referred to as the "heart" or the mind. Lastly, our spirit is the true essence of ourselves. It is the part of us that lives on after we die and is never asleep (Ecc. 12:7). It is the part of us that knows God and connects with Him, and it is also the part of us that conjugates the spiritual realm.

Now here is a *major* truth you must grasp and hold on to: before anything happens in the physical realm, it first originated in the spiritual realm. For example, if we study the creation story in Genesis chapter one, specifically verse 28, we can see that God blessed Adam and Eve and told them to be fruitful and multiply, but if we understand that God is Spirit (John 4:24), then His blessings are also spiritual. Adam and Eve could not achieve this blessing on their own before God spoke it in the supernatural.

Another example of blessings would be in the lives of Abram and Sarai in the book of Genesis, chapter 15. Here we see God making a promise and a covenant with Abram. God promised Abram that he would be the father of many nations, and he would have a son. The thing is, this promise did not come to pass for another ten years (Gen 21). Therefore, we understand that nothing can take place in the physical or natural realm without it first originating in the spiritual realm.

The Source of Dreams

In relation to dreams, understanding the spiritual realm and how it operates can give us a clue to understanding the mystery of dream and what source it came from. The type of dream we have is based heavily on the source and can originate from God, the enemy, ourselves, or externally.

Dreams from God

As we know, dreams are a *huge* way God speaks to us, but there's actually more to the equation. Did you know that there are different types of dreams from God? I know! As if the rabbit hole of cracking the dream code could get any deeper! So, before we get into those categories, I think it'll be helpful to understand *how* to discern if a dream is from God in the first place.

Dreams from God reflect His character, validate the Scriptures, are sometimes very detailed and colorful, and can have many seemingly random details or events.

To start, dreams from God echo His character, and the best way to know His character is through studying the Word of God. The Bible tells us that God is loving, just, merciful, gracious, compassionate, kind, patient, authoritative, convicting, righteous, and truthful to name a few. Thus, dreams from God will reflect who He has revealed about Himself in the Word of God.

Moreover, God dreams do not contradict the Scriptures because God does not go against His own Word. For example, let's take this Scripture when God was speaking to the nation of Israel.

Deuteronomy 13:1-3 New International Version (NIV)

1 If a prophet, or one who foretells by dreams, appears among you and announces to you a sign or wonder, 2 and if the sign or wonder spoken of takes place, and the prophet says, "Let us follow other gods" (gods you have not known) "and let us worship them," 3 you must not listen to the words of that prophet or dreamer. The Lord your God is testing you to find out whether you love him with all your heart and with all your soul.

Now let's say that someone has a dream, and in it, someone or something is trying to convince you to do something that is contradictory to God's commands. From what we just read in the Bible, we can conclude that it's probably a deceptive dream from the enemy and not a dream from God.

And if you're wondering if you have to read the *entire* Bible to know how to discern the source of the dream, I'd say, "no." Jesus once said that His sheep hear His voice (John 10:27) meaning that those who are children of God know their Father's voice. Even if you are a newly converted Christian, you can still train yourself to hear His voice by continually being a student of the Word of God and growing in intimacy with His Spirit. When you spend more time in fellowship with Him and become more accustomed to His voice, you will be able to discern anything that deviates from it. While interpreting dreams, you'll soon be able to detect when a dream is from God or another source. Similarly, no one studies fake designer bags; you study the real one so well that you can always spot a fake!

Lastly, many dreams from God are *super* detailed and colorful. You may be asking why that is and remember earlier (I hope you've been paying attention!) when I said that God is a masterful Poet and that almost a third of the Bible is poetry? Well if He is the Creator, He can certainly impress vivid dreams upon us! Think about it. God created the whole universe and everything we see in nature has been fashioned by Him. Honestly, no details are wasted with God, and everything He creates is purposeful. So when it comes to our dreams, I always say the wilder and more complex it is, the more likely it is a God dream! Sometimes when I decode really elaborate dreams, I'm always *sooo* in awe how God gives meaning to every detail that I may have otherwise overlooked or discarded because too much is happening. Ever been there? I'm sure you have, but don't give up on those types of dreams just yet because they seem completely random. Let's keep opening our minds up to God speaking to us this way.

Now without further ado, let's get into the different categories of God dreams! Through my experience interpreting dreams, I have been able to group most God dreams into these main categories. Keep in mind that this isn't an exhaustive list, but these are some key types to help you crack the dream code. Also, it is common for different types of these dreams to overlap in one dream.

- Insight dreams
- Past insight dreams
- Encouragement dreams
- Calling dreams
- Instructional dreams
- Directional dreams
- Deliverance dreams
- Healing dreams
- Prophetic dreams
- Warning dreams
- Prophetic warning dreams
- Correctional dreams
- Warfare dreams
- Commentary dreams
- Closure dreams

Insight Dreams

So, let's start with insight dreams. Sometimes we are entirely oblivious to what's happening in our lives and the lives of those around us; this is where insight dreams come in. God utilizes these dreams to tell us things we are too busy or not keen enough to understand while awake.

These dreams usually give deeper *insight* into a situation that is currently happening in the dreamer's life. Unlike past insight and prophetic dreams which we'll cover in a moment, these dreams have a sense of timeliness to them. Usually, these dreams involve current events or what's happening in your spiritual walk. Imagine praying to God about a certain situation in your life, and He answers you through a dream. Although God is gracious and will provide other means of confirmation, we often miss His answers when we don't take the time to decode our dreams.

For example, let's say you have a friend in real life, and you both hang out all the time. Well, what if you started having recurring dreams of seeing her curse your name to other people or when she's alone. Mind you, this girl is the sweetest thing in real life! This type of dream could be God revealing her heart to you and possibly cautioning you to keep your distance! She's probably jealous of you, but you would never know in real life. Can you see why it's so important to take your dreams seriously?? This right here is no joke!

Past Insight Dreams

Have you ever had dreams from your past and have always wondered what in the world they meant? Well, as with insight dreams, past insight dreams give you more clarity about something that happened in your past and sometimes how it is affecting your present. These dreams are usually easy to spot because they have some type of marker from the past such as an old residence, job, relationships, etc.

Sometimes people lump any dream they have about the past as demonic and think it is automatically a spirit of regression and backwardness attacking them. *Honeyyy, nooo.* We'll speak more about *how* to interpret dreams in the next part, but we always want to rely on the Holy Spirit first, check the context, and try to determine the source. Dreams are like a box of chocolate; you never know what you'll get, and we cannot apply the same "rules" for one dream as we do the next.

Now, an example of a past insight dream would be let's say there was a job opportunity from the past that you didn't get. At this point, you probably have another job and moved on, but you thought the previous job was the one you should've received. Maybe it was what you thought your ideal job would look like and deep down, you're still salty that it fell through. Well, you may receive a dream about what *really* happened to that job and maybe why God closed that door. The dream could reveal what was going on behind closed doors at that company, and in the dream, you would've been miserable being there. So, to you, it may have seemed like the perfect job, but God and His wisdom saw otherwise. This type of dream could give you clarity on that situation.

Another example would be recurring dreams of your childhood home. Maybe something traumatic happened in that home that you never dealt with, and God could show you how that connects with your life now. Maybe you developed certain behaviors and mindsets that you may think are normal, and the Lord will begin to show you the root of your problems and how everything is affecting you currently.

Encouragement Dreams

Encouragement dreams spark hope in situations of our lives and remind us that God is still in control. In real life, maybe you're wondering if you're on the right track or you've been doubting promises over your life. God can give you an encouraging dream to give you strength in circumstances.

I had a dream interpretation consultation recently and a young lady shared a dream with me. Within the dream, there was a man on the tv screen that told her she was allowed to stay because of her credit score. After walking her through the interpretation process, we discovered that this was an encouragement dream from God. The man represented God, and her credit score represented her integrity. He was basically telling her she had grace in an area of her life because of her moral character. In the dream, other women were in a waiting room but had to go because their credit score was low. This was juxtaposing the young lady and her integrity compared to other women who could not receive the same grace due to their low morale. It's amazing that God sees everything and acknowledges what we do in private!

Calling Dreams

So, everyone has a calling to do something, and it can show up as a symbol in dreams. Before I get too ahead of myself, let's break down what a "calling" is. A calling is the "Christianese" term to describe a role you are called to play in this life. People sometimes get calling and purpose mixed up, but they are different though they work together.

I'll explain the difference by using a pen as an example. When we look at a pen, we can see that it has different components to it. It may have a plastic covering, some ink, and maybe a lid. All these pieces would be the pen's *callings* that would give it the *purpose* to *write*. As Christians, we are all called to bring heaven on earth, but how we will do it will look unique for each individual based on that person's callings. Some people will look like pencils, markers, crayons, paintbrushes, etc., but we all have the same purpose to write.

I feel like this generation is obsessed with discovering their "purpose" and, in a way, we have overcomplicated what that means. I always say the best way to discover your purpose is by faithfully and consistently walking in your callings. I know you're probably yelling in your head, *But I've been trying to figure that out forever! How in the world do I know what I'm called to do?!*

I hear ya, and even more, God hears you! This is the reason why He sends calling dreams to us. Examples of calling dreams would include dreaming about singing, dancing, teaching, owning a business, becoming a professional, marriage, parenthood, being in ministry, writing books, mentoring, preaching, event planning, etc. These dreams usually repeat themselves to affirm that they are indeed clues from God, and it's not just something you made up.

Another aspect of calling dreams is that they sometimes include an impartation from another person who is a pioneer or figurehead in that area. For example, let's say God is calling you to ministry and you receive a dream with a certain minister you look up to teaching you about that ministry or giving you something of theirs. It could be that the mantle they carry for that ministry is being passed to *you*. Almost like a passing of the baton in track.

I'll give you another example. On a live Q&A I hosted about dream interpretation, someone said that they were having dreams of Tye Tribett, a famous Gospel singer. This person would have dreams that they would write music for Tye Tribett and he would sing it publicly. I automatically recognize that those were calling dreams to song write. What was interesting though is that person doesn't song write at the moment nor has she considered it in her future. This can happen with calling dreams because God knows us better than we know ourselves. He knows the gifts and talents that are within us, and He can help us to discover them. Who knows? Maybe this person will become a famous songwriter one day and create songs for big-name artists. *Wouldn't that be something?!*

All in all, sometimes we avoid our callings for many reasons, including fear, perception, money, lack of support, etc. Still, God will remind you of the different callings over your life through these types of dreams.

Instructional Dreams

Have you ever wanted something or wanted to do something, but you had no idea *how*?! Ugh, just thinking about it makes me so frustrated. Thank God for instructional dreams! Instructional dreams from God are dreams in which God gives you specific instructions or solutions to problems. I'm so glad we have a Heavenly Father that doesn't just watch us struggle but gives us advice to things we're completely stumped on. God gives us instructions, advice, ideas, or suggestions through these types of dreams.

Listen, if there was ever any type of dream that you should not overlook and it's this one. Right here. God has been known to give cures, advice on how to walk out callings, and business plans through these kinds of dreams. Yes, you heard me right. I said, "business plans!" Listen. Don't sleep (pun unintended)! People have become extremely wealthy from instructional dreams from God. Imagine. You have a dream that solves a problem, make a business, and then boom. You're set! Who wouldn't want that? *If you don't, don't tell me so that we can still be friends.*

There's one last thing I want to mention about these types of dreams. Sometimes it's easy to assume that these dreams will be the end all be all for us and that it will be the final say. Not necessarily. The Bible says that we only prophesy in part and we only see in part (1 Cor 13:9) meaning we don't always get the full picture.

I remember when I was starting my own hair care business, and I was so stuck on the formulation. It seemed like no matter what I tried, there was always an issue. Well throughout that journey, I would receive instructional dreams on how to formulate the products, and I thought that was it. Boom. There's the entire formulation. End of story. But nope. I would later find out that it was just a piece of the puzzle but not the entire puzzle itself. It was just a push in the right direction, but God wasn't going to do everything for me. I learned in that season that God wanted to partner with me; He wasn't a dictator. He wasn't going to give me the whole map from A to Z, but He wanted to walk with me at every step.

Directional Dreams

Do you ever feel like you're at a crossroads in your life or don't know where your life is going? Directional dreams bring more clarity to what direction your life is taking. These dreams usually involve transportation and travel.

For example, let's say you have a dream that you're driving on a smooth road, but then it gets bumpy or you begin to drive on a dirt road. This could signal that you are about to go through some discomfort in your life. This isn't always necessarily a bad thing and could still be a season of growth for the dreamer.

Another example would be making a U-turn in a dream. This could represent being redirected in the course of life.

Back then, these dreams would frustrate me because let's be real. Who likes having their plans change up? But it's important to embrace these types of dreams because we really don't know everything. The Bible says, *Trust in the Lord with all your heart, and do not lean on your own understanding. In all your ways acknowledge him, and he will make straight your paths (Proverbs 3:5-6 ESV)*. So directional dreams from God could imply a change for the better or a change for our own good.

Deliverance Dreams

Deliverance dreams are so liberating, and they symbolize being freed from something. Sometimes we are being spiritually attacked and we may be aware of it or not. In any regard, deliverance dreams usually involve you being delivered from something or someone.

Ever have a dream that you were being chased or harmed in some type of way? And then out of nowhere, someone saves you or some divine intervention happens? Yep. That, my friends, is the classic formula for a deliverance dream.

A very common example of this type of dream is when you're getting chased by something and then out of nowhere, you begin to fly! *Ain't that something?* Yeah, totally a deliverance dream! Or maybe one has a dream of being in a battle and then all of a sudden, someone defends the dreamer and fights off the opposing enemy? That could definitely be God fighting your battles and is a truly wonderful dream to have!

Healing Dreams

Healing dreams from God are dreams that point to healing in the dreamer's life. As someone who is involved in deliverance ministry (this is the ministry of healing and casting out demons), I can attest that everyone needs healing and deliverance, especially Christians. In the next section when we discuss dreams from demons, and we will discuss how demons are able to enter one's life and how demonic oppression can be revealed through dreams.

So what types of healing would a person go through one might ask. Well, some common types would be unforgiveness, rejection, hurt, offense, truly the list goes on.

If you are currently healing or God is calling you to heal from something, then you may have dreams of bathrooms or bodily fluid which we will discuss more in-depth later.

For example, let's say you're going through some internal issues. Perhaps you have some strong resentment towards your father and struggle to forgive him in your heart. You may have a dream of dare I say it—defecating! Now depending on if you're healing properly or not in the natural, this symbol would show up as defecating in a toilet or somewhere improper.

Maybe you're wondering why God would use stool to represent inner healing. Isn't there a... *nicer* way to describe healing? Well, let's think about it. Firstly, God created our bodies and their functions. We may be prude about bodily functions, but God is not. Secondly, God can speak our language, and He often does through dreams. Stool has transformed into colloquial terms to describe something bad, useless, or negative expression. Again, if defecating and stool represent inner healing, it should remind us that things we are getting healed from are negative, useless, and something that should be discarded.

Another example of healing would be let's you have been battling with negative thoughts and then have a dream of taking a shower. It could represent being *washed* with the Word of God (Eph 5:26) or being *washed* by the blood of Jesus Christ (1 John 1:7, 9). This could mean God wants to transform your mind, or He is calling you to a confession of sins and repentance.

Prophetic Dreams

Prophetic comes from the root word *prophecy*. *Prophecy* as a New Testament term comes from the Greek word *prophetia*, which means "to interpret the will of God" or "to foretell." Prophetic dreams do just that and reveal to the dreamer something that will transpire later.

Personally, I wish I understood the nature of dreams when I started dreaming more frequently. At the start of my dream journey, I had a couple of dreams that came to pass and then assumed *all* my dreams were prophetic. I only paid attention to dreams that I assumed could be literal and discarded the rest. *Nooo*. I believe through my ignorance and the devil playing on my naïveté, I was deceived through my dreams.

I recall a time when I just got saved that I used to dream about a guy I liked. There was one week I dreamt about him almost every day, and my dreams seemed like confirmation that we would be together in a relationship. **facepalm** Listen, don't judge me. We've all been there at some point in time and assumed our dreams were prophetic and confirmation of what our flesh wanted. In the next section when we discuss how to interpret dreams, we'll go over the importance of relying on the Holy Spirit for an interpretation. Because to be honest, if it was up to us, our flesh can lead us astray (it did for me)!

Since prophetic dreams are so varied and diverse, it would be impossible to name every type. Some examples, though, of prophetic dreams can include dreams of a future event coming to pass, walking in your purpose, and celebrating a future milestone or life event.

Warning Dreams

So, let's talk about warning dreams! God utilizes these dreams to inform us of what's pending in the spiritual realm. *Chiiiilllleeee listen! These warning dreams are not to be played with hence the word, "warning!"* When He gives us these dreams, we must take specific actions depending on the content of the dream. Usually, there is an element of time sensitivity and direction to take.

So, you may be wondering how one should approach these dreams when he or she has it. My first advice to you is DON'T PANIC!! Warning dreams are not set in stone hence why they have not happened yet. I want to remind you that God is not in the business of tricking us. If you ever receive a warning dream whether, for yourself or someone else, chances are you or that person can stop it from transpiring in the natural. Usually, the action to take for a warning dream is to simply follow the advice you receive from that dream. It may be to make a decision opposite to the bad one or simply to refrain from making the wrong choice.

I have heard of a story of a young woman who had a warning dream of her moving to a certain place. In the dream, she was driving and on her way to this place, but along the way she got stopped by a cop and thrown into jail. Although she was having second thoughts of moving after she had the dream, she went anyway. Needless to say, after moving to that area, she fell into the wrong crowd, got addicted to drugs, and was thrown into prison. *Whew! Listen... These dreams are no joke!* Had she taken heed to refrain from moving to that area, she could've saved herself the trouble.

Sometimes warning dreams can be about things that are currently happening or something in the future. God is a God of seasons and always involves His children on things to come. Sometimes you may have a warning dream that does not correlate with what is currently happening in your life. That is what I would call a prophetic warning dream.

I experience these types of dreams a lot, especially when I'm about to start on a life project. The first time I encountered this dream was when God was calling me to start a praise dance ministry on my university campus. Mind you, I had not fully committed to this call and merely considered it in my mind. Next thing you know, I had a dream that the dance team was up and running, but there were *sooo* many people at practice! And what's more, most of the college students who attended the practice were in party clothes! In the dream, I was a bit bamboozled by the scene, but I continued on with practice. As I would try to conduct the meeting, however, everyone kept talking and it was almost impossible to keep order! After a while, I got so flustered that I straight up asked who was not sent by God. To my surprise, almost the whole crowd raised their hand. I asked all of them to leave and continued with the practice.

Whew! When I tell you that warning dream helped me so much when I finally started the ministry! *Hmph!* That dream was a direct warning to guard the ministry and to be discerning of who really was there to serve God's Kingdom and who was just there to play. If I did not heed that warning, I would've been stressed out trying to run the praise dance ministry.

Other examples of warning dreams involve our intrapersonal relationships. A young lady once came to me with a dream about a young man she was interested in. Although she was very tempted, she had not told him about her feelings towards him and prayed about it first. In her dream, she dreamt that they had started dating, but he was very fickle towards her. He would act interested in one scene, but in the next scene act disinterested. The last part of her dream was the most startling. The dream had skipped to the future, and she was speaking to a friend. She was completely dismayed and told her friend that she was lucky to be single. It appeared that she ended up marrying that guy but was unhappy with how her life and marriage turned out with him. *Listen...* Sometimes I just have to thank God because He is all-knowing and is the Beginning and the End. God loved this young woman so much that He warned her that this gentleman is not even worth her time and involvement with him would only lead to heartbreak at the end. I don't know about you, but that's incredible!

Correctional Dreams

Correctional dreams are God dreams that correct us when we misstep or fall out of alignment. These types of dreams are pretty tricky for some folks because they are not always cute and might even involve demons. Now before you exit, hear me out. The Bible says that God corrects those He considers His child (Proverbs 3:12, Hebrews 12:6), so sometimes He will use dreams to correct us when we misstep or are going in the wrong direction. The reason I say demons can be in these types of dreams is because sometimes the cause of our disobedience is the influence of a demonic spirit.

I've interpreted a dream before (see the full interpretation in Examples), and in it was a girl who, throughout the whole dream, seemed to be on the side of the dreamer. By the end of the dream, the dreamer got in trouble with the Father of the house, and He took her to jail. The first instinct most would have is to rebuke the dream upon waking because of the assumption that it is a demonic dream. Once the dream was interpreted, it was a surprise to find out that it was a correctional dream straight from God. We would've rebuked the dream, but God rebuked the dreamer!

A classic template of a correctional dream would be seeing yourself willfully participate in something reckless, destructive, or irresponsible and reaping the consequences of it. For example, let's say you have a dream and you are driving recklessly in a car but get stopped by the police and receive a ticket. It could symbolize making reckless decisions in real life and God rebuking you for them.

Additionally, it's important to note your feelings *within* a correctional dream but not necessarily how you feel when you wake up. You may be wondering why especially when it seems like the most intuitive thing to do. Like I mentioned earlier, these dreams are usually not cute, honey. You may wake up feeling fearful or nervous, but is that how you were feeling within the dream? For example, I had a friend who came to me with a dream, and in it, she went to a wild party. Being there, she felt uncomfortable and thought to leave, but she lingered at this house party. Soon enough, a shootout happened, and she began to run for her life. Fast forward to the end of the dream and she spotted a yellow Lamborghini. She and a couple of people got in, but there was an old friend who was shot in the ear that was having difficulty getting in the car. Eventually, bad guys came and shot up the car she was in. *Whew! Babyyy...* That is not a good dream. When she woke up, she ruled out this dream as demonic, but when we peered deeper, it was definitely a correctional dream from God. First of all, if she knew she wasn't supposed to be at that party, why was she there and why didn't she leave when she got the conviction? Secondly, she was provided a means to escape but was trying to hold on to something from her past that could not go with her on this journey. Therefore, her fickleness and delay allowed an attack on her life.

Another example of a correctional dream I heard was a dream in which a woman went to the gas station to pump some gas. She wasn't paying attention and pumped too much. The gas spilled all over the floor to which the woman said, "oh well" and drove off. Again, most times correctional dreams will feature the dreamer doing something irresponsible (big or small). It's interesting because the dreamer's attitude was very nonchalant, and she didn't even attempt to clean up the mess. Not to mention, the gas only spilled out because sis wasn't paying attention. This could point to something she is neglecting in the natural that is reaping a negative consequence, and she has an uncaring attitude about it.

All in all, it's vital to take heed to correctional dreams. Let's not forget that there are true consequences to our disobedience, but God is so merciful. He won't see us slipping and turn a blind eye, but He lovingly guides us in our lives.

Warfare Dreams

Next, let's discuss warfare dreams. These dreams include fighting a battle of some sort. Depending on the dreamer or context, these dreams can feel exhilarating or terrifying! If you are ill-equipped, there may be a reason to worry. The Bible says in Ephesians 6:11 that our battle is not against flesh and blood meaning we are in a spiritual battle. Remember earlier when we discussed the spiritual realm? Well, warfare dreams usually indicate a spiritual battle that may manifest in reality.

A common setting of warfare dreams may include a war or apocalypse (end times). Let's say you have a dream of fighting in a war, but you have no weapon. *Yikes!* This may indicate that you are missing something vital in a battle that you are in, and what's missing is most likely the Word of God. You may be wondering why, so let's dissect that. In the Bible, there is a scripture that details the whole armor of God (Ephesians 6:10-18), and the Word of God is likened to a sword. As believers, our only offensive tool against the enemy is the Word of God. When we are lacking in our relationship with God and understanding the truth of the Word, we are unable to fight against the devil's schemes in our lives. Remember—it is so important to continue to be a student of the Word.

So, what are some other common warfare type dreams and what could they indicate for the dreamer? Well, warfare dreams usually center around the setting and who is involved. For example, let's say there was a fight or battle within a church. That may point to actual warfare within a church or ministry that the dreamer is part of or a battle in the dreamer's spiritual walk. Another example could be let's say a war against zombies. If we think about it, zombies are humans that should be dead, but they have risen from the dead. A dream like this could point to a generational curse/battle in the dreamer's life. Perhaps the dreamer has a destructive pattern within his or her family that is now trying to attack him or her.

When you receive dreams like this, don't panic. Sort through it to understand which area of your life this dream is referring to, and then go from there. The Holy Spirit is our guide!

Closure Dreams

I bet you've never heard of a closure dream before. Yeah. I made it up. But in all seriousness, closure dreams from God gives us closure in a situation (a bit redundant, but hey). Something I love about God is that He cares about our emotions and considers our reactions to different things. He will use these types of dreams to gracefully usher the dreamer through something ending. These dreams are usually peaceful, and there's an element of comfort that comes from them. For example, I have heard of people receiving dreams of a loved one passing away shortly before they died. Another example of a closure dream would be a friendship or partnership ending mutually.

Commentary Dreams

And lastly, we have commentary dreams. These are dreams in which Scripture is being revealed and the character of God is being exemplified. Sometimes in these dreams, you are merely observing the scene but usually not a partaker in it. For example, a friend came to me with a dream in which she was attending a wedding that was circus themed, and the wedding was very chaotic. The dream turned out to be a *commentary* about the Church (Ephesians 5:25-27, Revelation 19:7-9). God was showing her the current state of the worldwide Church, and it was possibly a prayer point as well.

Another friend of mine shared with me a dream she had about abortion. It was interesting because she was seeking God about His heart on the matter shortly before having that dream.

Lastly, as I mentioned, sometimes these types of dreams are scriptural. I remember a young lady who came to me with a long, elaborate dream, and when I sat down to interpret it, I couldn't believe how much Scripture was embedded into the dream. I mean almost every symbol and scene were literally bible verses jumping out at me. *God is so creative!*

Dreams from Demons

So, let's look into demonic dreams. Before we talk about demonic dreams, let's first discuss what demons are and the job of demons. Satan and his demons are fallen angels that were kicked out of heaven after Satan rebelled against God. The name *Satan* literally means "the adversary" in Hebrew, and the job of the enemy is to lead people away from the one true God.

Remember when we discussed where dreams come from earlier? As we mentioned, dreams are a monitor to the spiritual realm. Nothing manifests first in the natural realm without first originating in the spiritual realm, and the enemy knows that.

Let's take a look at a parable Jesus told in Matthew 13:24-28a [my emphasis added].

The Parable of the Weeds

*24 Jesus told them another parable: "The kingdom of heaven is like a man who sowed good seed in his field. 25 But while everyone was **sleeping**, his enemy came and sowed weeds among the wheat, and went away. 26 When the wheat sprouted and formed heads, then the weeds also appeared.*

27 "The owner's servants came to him and said, 'Sir, didn't you sow good seed in your field? Where then did the weeds come from?'

28 "'An enemy did this,' he replied.

Wow! The enemy Jesus spoke about in this parable was very smart and sowed seeds while everyone was sleeping. Likewise, we as human beings are the most vulnerable and unaware when we sleep. It is the perfect strategy for the enemy to plant negative seeds in our lives while we are deep slumber.

Without the practice of interpreting dreams, it would be difficult to identify the origin of a dream and where it originated. As mentioned before, demons can appear in all types of dreams including some God dreams and soul dreams. Not every bad dream is demonic and not every good dream is from God. Dreams are highly complex, but still, there are some ways to identify when a dream is demonic. Some clues that could indicate a dream is demonic are dull, muted, or dark colors; fewer details and sometimes quick dreams (compared to elaborate dreams God may give at times); and something is off, but you can't put your finger on it.

Before we dive deep into this topic, I want to mention that constant demonic dreams are not normal. I've noticed many people's ears perk up when it comes time to discuss demons, but my friends, this should not be the case. When you are a child of God and are faithfully chasing after Him, you should not continuously encounter demonic things (whether demons, nightmares, night terrors, or sleep paralysis)! Yes, there are many things we are ignorant of that the Lord will lovingly show us, but it is not in His nature to torment us with demons every single night. As we will soon discover, this only happens when we have an open door in our life that grants demons legal access.

I would also like to add that we must be willing to chase God—not just His answers and solutions. Too many of us want the healing and the deliverance, but we do not desire the Healer and Deliverer. So many people come to me with demonic dreams, and when I tell them what it means, to seek God, or fast and pray, they ignore it. *Like sis, why did you come to me in the first place?!* We can't just request a quick fix but reject eternal satisfaction. Yes, we can pray away demons through Jesus Christ's name, but we must work out our salvation through fear and trembling (Phil 2:12). Once we receive salvation, we must continue the work of sanctification by following Jesus and making Him Lord in our lives.

Now we got that out the way, let's discuss the two types of demonic dreams a person could have—overt or covert. Keep in mind that extra resources regarding how to combat demonic dreams will be in the Appendix.

Overtly Demonic Dreams

Overtly demonic dreams are dreams that the dreamer can clearly tell are evil. These are dreams where you clearly get attacked and wake up panicked, scared, or have physical markings on your body. Nightmares, night terrors, sleep paralysis, and dream rape all fall under the umbrella of overtly demonic dreams. These dreams should definitely be prayed against (or rebuked) upon waking, but these dreams often come about through an open door in your life.

Everyone has a basic hedge (or force field) of protection around them, as we see in Job 1:10. If it weren't for this, we would be continuously tormented night and day. When we have an open door in our lives, it creates a hole in our hedge for demons to find their way into our lives. This is what we call a *legal right*.

Let me tell you a little bit about the kingdom of darkness (by the way, I will be using the terms kingdom of darkness, the enemy, and demons interchangeably throughout this book, so be forewarned). Y'all, the enemy is a whole legalist! That means he knows the rules, and he exploits it! Satan knows the Bible we read front and back and has found every loophole to achieve his ultimate goal— draw mankind away from the Creator. When we read the first two chapters of the book of Job, we see something interesting. Satan could not harm Job without the consent of God. Now although Satan had a goal, homie still had to get permission from God to carry out his plan. *Ain't that somethin'?!* It goes to show that Satan is not the opposite of God. He literally has no real power and can only inflict harm at the sovereignty of God and man's own free will.

Moreover, the bible says that a curse causeless shall not come (Prov 26:2), meaning there is always a root to a curse. Everyone gets attacked in dreams from time to time because since we are friends to God, we are a threat to Satan and his kingdom. But still, constant demonic dreams are not normal and usually indicate an open door the enemy has legal access to.

Let's explore some common open doors, and in the Appendix, we'll discuss how to shut them.

Willful sin

So, let's talk about sin but not just any kind of sin. We're talking willful sin, aka transgression and iniquity. *Whoa there.* Those were a lot of Christianese terms, so let's define them, shall we?

Firstly, sin just means missing the mark. Imagine throwing a dart at a bullseye, and you miss. That's what sin looks like. Sin, in general, is an umbrella for every type of sin—knowingly and unknowingly. You may be wondering how someone could sin unintentionally, and that act would still be considered a sin. Well, we were all born into sin, and we live in a fallen or imperfect world, so no one is without sin. The only person to walk this earth without sin was Jesus Christ which is why He was the perfect sacrifice for our sins (2 Corinthians 5:21). Now before I get too much ahead of myself and start to go down the rabbit hole of theology, I'll give you an example of an unintentional sin in the Bible. In Numbers 35, there were whole guidelines given to the nation of Israel on how to handle a murder. If we pay attention, we also see that there were also guidelines for dealing with manslaughter. Even if it was accidental, manslaughter was still considered a sin that defiled the land, so therefore that is what we call an unintentional sin.

Let's talk about transgression now. This is a deeper sin that a person willfully participates in. Let's imagine a boundary line that separates two things, and now envision someone cognitively overstepping that line that was set. That, my friends, is what transgression looks like. For example, abusing another image-bearer is willful sin. That person is fully and cognitively aware that what they are doing is wrong even if they try to convince themselves otherwise (and we're not just talking about personalities). When we deliberately defile God's commandments to love Him with all our heart, soul, and strength; and love our neighbors as we love ourselves (Mark 12:30-31), then we commit a transgression.

Lastly, let's discuss iniquity. *Now, this is some big boy stuff!* Iniquity is willful, continually, and unrepentant sin. Iniquity is usually developed when a person's heart becomes hardened to the correction of God. *Whew! You really don't want this, big fella.* It's one thing if a person engages in a transgression once, but all the time?! That's a recipe for demons.

All in all, willful sin is the first gateway for demons in someone's life. Defying God's basic commands to love Him and love your neighbor, engaging in criminal activities, and using illicit drugs are just some ways demons can access a person and can inevitably induce overtly demonic dreams.

Illegal Sex

Whew! Now, this right here! By far, one of the easiest access points devils use. Illegal sex is any type of sex or sexual acts outside the covenant of marriage between a man and a woman. This includes (but is not limited to): fornication, premarital sex, adultery, incest, pedophilia, homosexual acts, bestiality, masturbation, and pornography.

The Bible says that when a man leaves his family and *cleaves* to his wife, then the two will become one *flesh* (Genesis 2:24, Matthew 19:5, Mark 10:8, Ephesians 5:31). *Listen...!* If the Bible repeats something multiple times, it's definitely something we should pay attention to! Becoming one flesh does not just mean physically coming together sexually, but there is a *soul tie* that takes place. Although the Bible does not mention the term "soul tie," the concept is still there (just like the Trinity). Soul ties were created by God and served a godly purpose, but of course, Satan perverted it. Godly soul ties include relationships between husbands and wives, parents and children, and godly friendships (1 Samuel 18:1). An ungodly soul tie would involve intimate relations with unbelievers (2 Corinthians 6:14-16); relationships born from abuse, manipulation, or control (Genesis 34:1-3); and any act of infidelity (1 Corinthians 6:16).

When we defile the marriage bed (Hebrews 13:4), we open the door for demons to enter. Let's say we have a woman named Angela, and Angela struggles with a spirit of depression. Angela now has premarital sex with a man named Jacob. Jacob then fornicates with another woman named Mercy. So now, Mercy has a spirit of depression all the way from Angela, who she has no relation to! *STDS, aka sexually transmitted demons, are no joke.* This might seem extreme for some people, but I have seen this time and time again in deliverance ministry. God created sex and sees it as a good thing. The enemy now comes in to pervert a precious gift from God for his own agenda.

So, we've talked about illegal sex being a gateway to demons, but how would this manifest in an overtly demonic dream? Usually, this open door can show up as sex in dreams. Depending on the person's exposure to sex, they may enjoy it or feel as if they are being raped in their dream. I have heard reports of people getting raped by demons, and they actually felt penetration. **shudders* This ain't it, chief.*

Even if you are a "virgin," you can still have demons come to you and have sex in your dreams. Demons don't care if someone has had actual penetration; they can still plant seeds of perversion through dreams and can cause people to masturbate or watch porn. In a deliverance session recently, a young lady was a virgin but struggled with masturbation throughout her life. We soon found out that this young lady had a *spirit spouse*! *Yikes!* So, a spirit spouse is basically what it sounds like. A demon that is married to you in the spirit realm. The function of a spirit spouse is to plant seeds of perversion, lust, and keep people from having fruitful marriages. This young lady may have thought she was just pleasing herself through masturbation, but in fact, she was feeding this demon. *Ugh! Demons are so icky.*

Last example, and then I'm done scaring you. As much as this may be alarming for you, it's even more uncomfortable for me to type it. Okay, so I knew of this one young lady in college who shared that since she was a little girl, she always had a merman come and have sex with her every night in her dreams. *ICK!* Now for the normal Westerner that may be reading this, that doesn't seem suspicious. Without going too much into demonology and culture, mermaids and sirens are what are called *marine spirits*. Marine spirits are demons that have some type of rule over the sea. Throughout history and folklore, mermaids are depicted as seductive, mythical creatures that lure people out to sea. There is actually some truth to this, but they are not the fun Ariel of *The Little Mermaid* that may come to mind. These are demonic spirits and may be connected to spirit spouses.

To recap, when a person has illegal sex, they can create an open door for demons to enter into their life. That open door may reflect through dreams in a number of different ways, so be mindful. If you read all of this with conviction, I tell you to not be afraid. Demons are wimps and have already been overcome by Jesus Christ! If you fell in the past, you can get back up and keep going. Don't let the devil intimidate you and make you feel hopeless. The Bible says, "There is therefore now no condemnation to those who are in Christ Jesus, who do not walk according to the flesh, but according to the Spirit (Romans 8:1)." Any mistake you made has been forgiven when you repented of your sins. *And that's on period!*

Generational Curses

Generational curses are destructive behaviors and patterns that are passed on from generation to generation. Generational curses, for the most part, are easy to spot. Take a look at your family right now. Do you notice an unhealthy pattern within your bloodline? You may notice that all the men in the family struggle with alcohol, or everyone struggles with poverty, or you may see a pattern of single motherhood. All these are examples of generational curses.

You may wonder why this is even a thing at all. Well, let's see what the Bible has to say!

Exodus 20:4-6 New International Version (NIV) (emphasis added)

4 "You shall not make for yourself an image in the form of anything in heaven above or on the earth beneath or in the waters below. 5 You shall not bow down to them or worship them; for I, the Lord your God, am a jealous God, ***punishing the children for the sin of the parents to the third and fourth generation of those who hate me,*** *6 but showing love to a thousand generations of those who love me and keep my commandments.*

Wow! This Scripture occurred when the Lord God gave the Ten Commandments to the nation of Israel. As we can see from the text, God punishes the sins of parents up to the third and fourth generation! What does that mean? That means if your ancestor participated in some type of iniquity, demons have the legal right to visit the descendants with the same torment. *Chaiii...! Sorry o. Sometimes the Nigerian in me has to come and express itself!*

So, if you have a generational curse, it can definitely show up in your dreams. Demonic dreams that may indicate a generational curse are dreams of a deceased relative talking to you, passing along some information, or giving you a gift. Some other symbols would include dreams of ancestors or getting initiated to participate in some type of family/generational tradition. Most of the time, generational curses show up covertly in dreams which we will talk about shortly.

The Occult

So, occultism is not something that is easy to summarize in one neat category. Although there are different types of occultism, they can all be described as "hidden, secret, and pertaining to the supernatural." I know. That was so basic. But that's what makes the occult alluring to many people. We want to harness power, revelation, and secrets without God. This, my friends, is what makes the occult so dangerous and deceptive. It may *seem* harmless and for many people, it may actually work! The problem lies in the *source* of the occult which is always demonic. God did not condemn the occult throughout Scripture because it *wouldn't* work. He cursed it because it *does* work, but it is deception, inspired by demons, and leads His children away from Him.

Before I continue, let me backtrack to some examples of the occult.

Occultism includes (but is not limited to):

- Astrology & horoscopes (Isaiah 47:13-14)
- Witchcraft (traditional religions, juju, voodoo, Santeria, obeah, black and white magic, etc.)
- New Age rituals (yoga, astral projections, levitation, chanting, sage smudging, charms, crystals, tarot cards, etc.)
- Necromancy (that is, consulting the dead)
- Visiting mediums, psychics, palm readers, tarot card readers, spiritists, etc. (Leviticus 19:31)
- Secret societies (Freemasonry, Eastern Star, college fraternities & sororities, etc.)

See, the problem with all these things is seeking power outside God and His will. Remember earlier when I mentioned that there are only two kingdoms—the kingdom of light and the kingdom of darkness? Yep. There is no in-between in the spirit realm no matter how innocent or harmless it seems. Multiple times in the Bible the Lord clearly said that if you mess with these things, they will *defile* you! It's interesting that the word "defile" is used because it denotes making something *unclean*. In the New Testament, Jesus refers to demons as unclean spirits (Matthew 12:43), so therefore we can conclude that participating in the occult can introduce demons into one's life.

I do want to mention that demons can visit someone even if that person did not participate in the occult. When we spoke about generational curses, I mentioned how demons can visit the descendants of those who commit iniquity. For example, let's say you have a grandparent that participated in witchcraft. Although *you* have not personally touched it, there is a legal right the enemy can enter in from. In many deliverance cases I've seen, I noticed that it is very common for demons to attack other family members when one member of the family has engaged in the occult.

In the dream realm, a manifestation of occultism can include sleep paralysis; someone forcing you to eat something such as a potion, bugs, worms, rotten or spoiled food; drinking blood or dirty water; seeing your name on an altar such as a table with candles, an initiation table, a grave, in the sea, or in a tree; and hearing others chant your name.

These types of dreams are nothing to mess with! When I tell you that the enemy is a legalist and will find any loophole to gain access, *chileee... I'm not playin'!* Fortunately, Jesus Christ already conquered the devil and has given us the authority to do so as well!

Other Common Open Doors

So, there are *wayyy* too many open doors to go through in this one book, and I'm certain you want to get to the good stuff already! Trust me, I'm not going through all this to scare you, but I want you to be aware of the strategies of the enemy. Any who, you're probably getting bored or scared with all this demon talk, so I'll wrap this section up.

Below are some other common open doors which can cause demonic dreams:

- Unforgiveness (Matthew 18:21-35)
- Spoken curses (Proverbs 18:21)
- False religions (any religion that claims Jesus is not the only way to the Father and Heaven)
- Cursed objects (idols, statues of other deities, charms, crystals, objects used in witchcraft or the occult, accursed objects from foreign countries with spirits tied to them)
- Cursed places (living or sleeping in a place with territorial demons or monitoring spirits; a place with a pattern of something wicked like illegal sex, homicides, suicides, drugs, etc.)
- Abuse (physical, psychological, verbal, mental, or sexual)
- Addiction (alcohol, marijuana, heroin, cocaine, any form of gluttony)

Some other overtly demonic symbols include:

- Getting stabbed, shot at, or bitten
- People stealing from you

Covertly Demonic Dreams

Now that's out of the way, let's discuss something more juicy—covertly demonic dreams! So, what are they? Covertly demonic dreams are dreams in which demons use different types of deception to manipulate the dreamer into accepting whatever device they are trying to plant in that person's life. Overtly demonic dreams are easy to spot because they are very conspicuous, but covert dreams are a bit more sinister. Usually, covert dreams involve masquerading and familiar spirits, which we will discuss further in the character section. In essence, these dreams have a sense of familiarity in them, but something is extremely off. Have you ever experienced something like that before? Like a situation where everything seems right on the surface, but there's something wrong and you can't put your finger on it. Many times, these could be covertly demonic dreams!

With dreams like this, we often brush them off because if we don't understand something, we just rationalize it away. Friend, we got to do better! Ignoring these dreams can have major consequences and that gives the dream permission to materialize in real life! I know it still seems a bit vague now, but the Bible says to be alert and of sober mind, because our enemy, the devil, is always on the prowl (1 Peter 5:8)!

A key thing to look for in covertly demonic dreams is the *feel* of a dream. Does it seem like a normal or good dream, but for some reason, it feels off? This could be a clue that the dream may be deceptive. Do you see someone or people that you are familiar with, but something is off? Is a person taller, shorter, bigger, slimmer, or just acting in a way that they normally wouldn't in real life? This could point to *masquerading* or *familiar spirits*. In essence, these spirits pretend to be someone or something the dreamer is familiar with to gain trust and ultimately deceive the person. If we think about it, this is a very good tactic. If a devil came to us in their true form, we would immediately be able to spot a spiritual attack. But what if the enemy came to you as a parent or a friend? You would be more likely to trust what's happening because you trust the person.

You may be wondering why and how could a demon pretend to be something that is *good*? Well in the Scriptures, Satan is said to masquerade as an angel of light (2 Corinthians 11:14), so demons can shapeshift into "good" things too. Now although demons use this tactic often in covertly demonic dreams, they are not very good at it, in my opinion. You would think after all this time they would've mastered the art of imitation but, no. They suck. When a demon pretends to be someone you know in a dream, there's always something off!

I recall a dream I had some time ago. Someone gave me a message to tell my friend, and in the dream, I went to tell her. As I was about to give her the message, my close guy friend (who was actually a demon in the dream) started yelling at me! And for something so stupid and nonsensical at that. Later in the dream, he came back to me, and when I tell you this man's nose was so big! I was utterly confused in the dream, and I was asking him why his nose was so big. He literally looked like the wicked witch from the west in the Wizard of Oz. Mind you, when I woke up I completely forgot the message I was supposed to tell my friend. I guess in this instance they achieve their goal.

Let me give you another example of a familiar spirit working in a covertly demonic dream. A friend of mine used to constantly have negative dreams of her mother. One particular dream she had was of her and her mother leaving somewhere. As they were leaving, her mother said something incorrectly in their native language that she would never mess up in real life. In the dream, my friend called it out and said, "You're not my mother." To that, her "mother" looked at her with shock, and then she woke up. *shaking my head* Demons really think they're slick! This specific dream opened her eyes to how demonic entities were trying to pit her against her mother.

I'll give you one more example of a covertly demonic dream, and hopefully, this will all make sense to you. So I had a dream in which I was at home. I was sweeping in the kitchen and my mother was speaking loudly on the phone (if you're Nigerian, you know it's our culture). Out of the blue, I *remembered* that I got engaged *two* weeks ago. I looked on my *right* hand and noticed two rings on my finger. One was gaudy which I assumed was one he gave me when we were friends, and then a daintier engagement ring on top. I pulled out my phone and noticed that I had not spoken to my fiancé in a bit because it seemed like we got in a creative discussion (**cough cough* an argument*) through our last messages. I also saw a snap from Snapchat when he proposed to me. It was me, him, and his mother. Interesting. Lastly, I realized that I had not told anyone, not even my closest friends, about the engagement! As I went into our friend group, I was typing out that I got engaged then woke up.

Hmph. To the naked eye, that *looks* like a good dream, and I was almost fooled. I knew something was off, but I couldn't put my finger on it. The first thing I did was look up which finger the engagement ring was supposed to go on (I didn't know at that time), and it was the *left* hand. Now I was really interested! Although I didn't know enough about dreams at the time, the more I grew in dream interpretation, the more I pondered on this dream.

For one, why was my mother there even though she didn't add anything to the dream? I was able to conclude that it wasn't my mother but a demonic familiar spirit. The spirit masqueraded as my mother to make me feel comfortable in the dream and accept what was happening. *Nice try, buddy!* The next thing that struck me as funny is how did I *forget* that I got engaged?! That's a huge life event that I would not forget in two weeks. Next, the rings were placed on the wrong hand. They almost got me with that one if I hadn't looked it up (because I knew something was fishy). Lastly, how in the world did my close friends not know I was engaged for TWO WEEKS?! *How sway?* Nah. They almost got me, but the joke is on them.

I know I didn't go through every symbol, but the main gist is that this was a covertly demonic dream specifically as an attack on my future marriage. Listen. The devil knows that when two believers come together in the covenant of marriage, it spells disaster for his kingdom. The reason the enemy uses covertly demonic dreams is that it's discreet. Trust me. If that dream was overtly demonic, I would've destroyed his plans sooner! *Jùmòké does not play!* Since this was a covertly demonic dream, it took me months to realize what the enemy was doing.

Although there are so much more examples, here are other possibilities of a covertly demonic dream:

- Deceased loved ones giving you something
- Friends encouraging you to participate in demonic activities
- Someone giving you something questionable
- A person you're attracted to having sex with you

Sleep Paralysis

If you have ever experienced sleep paralysis, you can probably testify that it was a frightening experience! Sleep paralysis is an unfortunate phenomenon when people are caught in a hazy space where they're not asleep, but they are not fully awake either. In this twilight zone of sorts, many people record feeling pinned to the place they're resting, unable to move, seeing demons, and sometimes unable to speak.

Unfortunately, I cannot give you a solid reason why this happens. For me, I have only encountered this twice in my walk, and that was within the first couple of months I got saved. I was never scared, though. I would force myself out of it by saying the name "Jesus" then go into spiritual warfare or pray out scripture.

A friend of mine suffers constantly from sleep paralysis which she just discovered was linked to generational demons and witchcraft put on her. Through this knowledge, she was able to target her prayers and counter the attacks.

I have some theories about sleep paralysis, though. I believe this can be caused by an open door (as we mentioned) or the enemy could be using it as a tool to scare and torment people. If someone has a powerful gift of seeing (seeing into the spiritual realm) or is prophetic, the enemy may attempt to intimidate that person. Once a person curses that gift, they may stop seeing and dreaming altogether which is what the enemy wants. In any regard, if you are someone who suffers from sleep paralysis and they are constant, it's time to fight back and grow in your spiritual walk.

Here are some tips to overcome sleep paralysis (more empowerment will be in the Appendix):

- Ask the Lord to reveal to you what open doors are these occurrences happening from
- Be open to how the Lord may reveal the answer (the Bible, YouTube, another believer, a minister, a deliverance ministry, etc.)
- Pray against the attack, but not the gift of seeing itself
- Continuously grow in your relationship with God

Dreams from Ourselves

Dreams from ourselves are referred to as *soul dreams*. To recap, we, as human beings, consist of a spirit, soul, and body. Some say mind, body, and soul; but spirit, soul, and body are more accurate. Since your soul houses your thoughts, will, and emotions, soul dreams often reveal internal struggles you are currently facing. Amazingly, God can still speak to you through these types of dreams.

I want to mention the importance of not throwing away soul dreams. It seems intuitive to discard these types of dreams because they are not from God or demonic, but we should pause to reflect on them. Sometimes, soul dreams reveal what's going on internally if we were unable to perceive it in the natural. Personally, I welcome soul dreams because it helps me to become more introspective and honest with myself. I'm able to see how certain things affect me as they manifest through my dreams.

I recall a few years back I had a falling out with someone. Although I thought I was over it, I would have many dreams of me fighting this person. And I mean *fight*. I'm a small woman, so I was even surprised I could fight like that. Those dreams were revealing to me the anger I still had towards this person, and I needed God to heal me from the hurt. I also noticed that when others came to me with similar dreams, fighting someone represented inner anger, resentment, hate, or unforgiveness towards another.

Another example of a soul dream I interpreted was one of a young lady. She shared a dream with me of her carrying a baby who happened to be her. She was telling the baby all the mistakes of her past and how to avoid them. This was a soul dream that was revealing the regrets she had of her life. If she could go back in time, there are many things she would've done differently.

The last example of soul dreams revolves around a fictional situation. Have you ever been in a confrontation or argument with someone but for some reason, you couldn't find the words to say at that moment? Sometimes your brain will rehash the situation via a soul dream. You may find yourself reliving a current situation with a different outcome. Maybe there's something you want to tell someone but you may not have the guts to do it in real life so you end up dreaming about it. This is a case of a soulish dream.

Examples of soul dreams:

- Running away, but nothing is chasing you
- Falling
- Seeing yourself willfully participate in something you wouldn't or couldn't do normally do in real life

External Dreams

External dreams involve dreams induced externally or out of the body. So, taking some medications can, at times, evoke external dreams/hallucinations. Being under the influence of marijuana, alcohol, and other drugs can affect your dreams. Be aware of the state you are in before you go to sleep to determine if a dream has been induced externally.

Lucid Dreaming

During my time as a dream interpreter, I've received many questions about lucid dreaming. Questions such as, "Can a Christian lucid dream?" and "Is lucid dreaming safe?"

First, let's discuss what lucid dreaming is. Lucid dreaming is simply the awareness that one is dreaming within a dream. If you've ever noticed that you are in a dream while you're physically asleep, then you have had a lucid dream.

There's nothing inherently wrong with lucid dreaming as most people have had at least one lucid dream in their lifetime. I even had a few dreams when in it, I was cognitively aware that I was in a dream, and I would even decode the symbols of the dream while they happened! The problem occurs with the *fascination* of it and the tie to New Age occultism. In an effort to gain total control over one's spiritual life, many New Agers engage in practices to provoke lucid dreaming. Through lucid dreaming, New Agers report visiting other galaxies, interacting with spirit guides and encountering other spiritual things. What many don't realize is that this opens up spiritual portals and exposes the spirit to different things. When lucid dreaming is evoked by anything other than the Holy Spirit, demons have legal rights into one's life because the person has engaged in divination.

The act of *provoking* lucid dreaming is a form of divination, sorcery, and idolatry. This opens up demonic doors in one's life and should be avoided. You may be wondering, *So, I've had lucid dreams completely by accident. What does that mean for me?* As mentioned earlier, accidental lucid dreaming is mostly harmless, and if the Holy Spirit provokes it, even better! I know with all the talk I just did about lucid dreaming, some people may be confused about how I could see it as a good thing.

Before we discuss that, I want to mention that in biblical times, people didn't distinguish between dreams and visions in the sense of hierarchy. They regarded both with high respect and took them seriously. As mentioned previously, visions are basically dreams you have while awake. Back then, prophets would have dreams and visions in which the Holy Spirit would transport them places or show them things.

Let's look at an example with prophet Ezekiel:

Ezekiel 8:1-3 New International Version (NIV)

"In the sixth year, in the sixth month on the fifth day, while I was sitting in my house and the elders of Judah were sitting before me, the hand of the Sovereign Lord came on me there. 2 I looked, and I saw a figure like that of a man.[a] From what appeared to be his waist down he was like fire, and from there up his appearance was as bright as glowing metal. 3 He stretched out what looked like a hand and took me by the hair of my head. The Spirit lifted me up between earth and heaven and in visions of God he took me to Jerusalem, to the entrance of the north gate of the inner court, where the idol that provokes to jealousy stood."

As we can see, Ezekiel's vision and transportation to the temple were elicited by the Holy Spirit which is a good thing. I believe these things still happen today, so if you find yourself in a similar situation, then it could be the Lord trying to show you something. The biggest caution I can give as far as lucid dreaming is not to seek ways to summon them yourself. Again, that is a form of divination.

Preparing to Dream

So, we've spoken so much about dreams themselves, but what about the actual act of dreaming? It's very common for some people to say that they don't dream. This may be true, but I believe it's for a few reasons.

For one, it is a scientific fact (if you don't trust me, then maybe you'll trust the research) that everyone dreams even a few times a night, but for most people, the problem is *remembering*. If you are someone who falls into this category, the best advice I can give is to invite God to speak to you through your dreams and create a good atmosphere to sleep in. Many times, the reason we don't remember our dreams is because we have lousy sleep hygiene or are dealing with a lot mentally. If you are someone that doesn't get enough rest or good enough rest, it will affect your dreaming. Also, if you are struggling with insomnia, worry, anxiety, or depression, these issues can take a toll on your ability to dream.

On the other hand, there are still some who were probably able to dream at a certain point in time but then stopped dreaming altogether. If you are someone who has the gift of seeing into the spiritual realm and dreaming but cursed it because you may not have been too fond of what you were seeing (*I feel you*), this can lock up that gift. The Bible says that the power of life and death lies in the tongue (Prov 18:21), so we must be careful about what we bless and what we curse. God gave us the ability to see and dream for

His glory and also for Him to communicate with us. What ends up happening is that sometimes the enemy will try to corrupt that gift to intimidate you from dreaming and seeing. If this is you and you had a bad experience with dreaming, I would encourage you to ask God to reopen that gift for you. I would also encourage you to pray and ask the Holy Spirit how to discipline this gift so that it can continue to grow.

Also, some of us are active dreamers, but from time to time, we go through a drought of not dreaming or remembering. I have experienced this many times in my walk, and this is attributed to what I call *dream snatchers* (you have to credit me on being creative with these names though). Dream snatchers are spirits sent to steal dreams or distract the dreamer from receiving revelations through their dreams. When we think about the importance of dreams and how the job of the enemy is to steal, then this plot would make sense. There would be times during my walk that I am dreaming nonstop, recording and interpreting my dreams and then—blank. All of a sudden, it seems as if my ability to remember gets switched off. As hard as I tried, I could not remember my dreams for the life of me! This confusion would usually go on for some days before I catch on to the plan of the enemy and rebuke the dream snatcher spirit. Almost immediately, I am able to remember my dreams again. If that has happened to you, then I would encourage you to go into spiritual warfare and counter the attack. Snatch back what the dream snatcher has stolen from you!

Lastly, some of you only dream from time to time, but maybe not often enough for you to say you have the gift of dreaming. Sometimes this happens because you are not stewarding over this ability properly. If God would like to speak to us through dreams, it is our job to go seek out the meaning of our dreams. God is not getting off His throne to spoon-feed us, and we must do our due diligence and seek the face of God. We cannot be content in having dreams and not even asking God for meaning. Too many of us throw away our dreams and we don't seek to understand what it could mean if God is, in fact, speaking to us. If this is the same God that spoke the universe into existence, how much more seriously should we take our dreams?

Sleep Hygiene

Now let's discuss the way we sleep which can affect our dreaming. Our environment, state-of-mind, and amount of sleep can influence the way we dream.

Taking Care of Your Space

One way to improve your dreaming is to ensure your environment is comfortable before you sleep and is a place the Holy Spirit can dwell. You may be wondering if there are places Holy Spirit *can't* dwell in. Well, the Holy Spirit resides in each born again believer. Although He can be *everywhere*, He isn't in *every* place. For example, the presence of God can be felt in let's say a church versus at a club. Let's imagine the Holy Spirit as a physical person.

Ask yourself—would *you* invite Him into the place you rest your head every night? If the answer is no, why is that?

Sometimes how we keep our space says a lot about us spiritually. When I enter some areas, I can tell if there are spirits of poverty, anxiety, depression, or fear simply by the way a person keeps their space. Many of us don't realize how much our environment affects us mentally and spiritually. For me, God revealed how my room was creating cycles of laziness, poverty, delay, and regression in my life, which consequently showed up as symbols in my dreams. As a clutter bug, I didn't realize my room and unhealthy habits contributed to feelings of anxiety and hopelessness in my life. Once I organized my room and developed productive habits, I was able to be and sleep in peace. Although my story is entirely subjective, I still believe that there is wisdom anyone can pull.

For you, incorporating some of these tips may help improve your environment before you sleep:

- Worshipping and praying in that area
- Inviting God to speak to you in dreams through prayer
- Tidy up your space before you sleep
- Have a consumption curfew. Cut off social media, worldly music, and tv before you sleep
- Play praise and worship music to set the atmosphere before bed
- Try reading the Bible before going to sleep

Taking Care of Your Mind

The next component of sleep hygiene is our state-of-mind before we sleep. Going to bed with negative feelings can limit dreams all together or invoke soul dreams. As we mentioned earlier, not all soul dreams are wrong, and some are necessary to give us crucial information about ourselves.

In waking life, if we are fighting with others, watching illicit things, and even going through trauma, these things can manifest in our dreams. We may receive nightmares or soul dreams from the different things we are currently experiencing. Mental illness such as depression, anxiety, or insomnia can also restrict our dreaming, and it is vital to seek God on the best matter to combat these issues and possibly consult a professional. Definitely check out more resources in the Appendix to fight these things.

Here are some practical tips to improve your state-of-mind before you sleep:

- Pray
- Journal your thoughts
- Stop working by a certain time. Don't take your work in bed with you.
- Find a stress-free activity to do before bed. Perhaps playing a calming game can relieve stress
- Enjoy a loved one's company

Taking Care of Your Body

Lastly, you want to make sure you're getting ample rest in order to dream and remember accurately. Adults need about six to eight hours of sleep a day, but most of us get significantly less. If that's you, consider getting more sleep and going to bed on time. I know everyone has different schedules and lifestyles but think about it as an investment to your health. The problem with not having enough sleep is that your REM sleep becomes interrupted. REM stands for rapid eye movement, and that is the stage of sleep where we have the most dreams. Being awakened from REM sleep due to perhaps an alarm clock can cut dreaming short, or the dreamer may forget all together due to the alarm waking him or her up suddenly. Being uncomfortable when you sleep can also affect the duration and quality of your sleep. For me, I *hateee* being hot when I sleep. I toss and turn to the point that when I wake up, I feel like I didn't even sleep. For you, it may be itchy clothes, being too cold, or awkward bedding. To cultivate your ability to dream, you want to ensure you are getting enough rest and are comfortable when you sleep.

How to Record Dreams

There are different ways to record dreams, but the most common ones are journaling, audio recording, and typing. When it comes to recording your dreams in general, it is so important to do this when you *first* wake up so that you do not forget! And when I say first, I mean first! Before you hop on your phone to check social media and other notifications. It is too common of an occurrence to receive a dream, check your phone, take a shower, eat breakfast, and before you know it, you've forgotten most details of your dream! Listen, it's just better, in the long run, to jot down your dreams when you wake up.

So, the first way to record dreams is by writing them down. Most dreamers have a dream notebook that they keep near their bed so that they can jot down all the essential details they dreamt about.

Some dreamers like to record their dreams audibly on their phones when they receive a dream. This method is great but may not be the best if you have a roommate or are married because you may wake them up! Use your discretion or record upon waking.

For me, I have personally enjoyed typing out my dreams on the Note app on my phone. Besides the screen light bothering my eyes when I want to record a dream in the middle of the night, this method of recording has worked the best for me. I have remedied that by dimming the screen brightness to its lowest setting before I go to bed and using Dark Mode on my phone. My favorite feature of this method is the fact that I can type in any keyword, and all the dreams with that keyword will pop up. For someone who dreams almost every single night, this has been the most convenient method for me as I can find old dreams quickly.

Remembering Dreams

Ever have a dream in which you could only pick up a few details? This phenomenon is very common, but what should we make of this? Well, there have been many times that I or others have only remembered the main parts of a dream, and there was still a considerable revelation to be gleaned. If you have a dream and only remember select details, I would still advise you to jot down whatever you can remember and attempt to interpret it. Sometimes, God, being so gracious, will give us another dream building upon the previous one. And if all else fails, you can always ask God to bring details back to your remembrance.

You may be wondering if it's okay to discount an entire dream because you don't remember all the details. *Nooo.* Still jot it down and take a crack at it. Even if it's just a few details, I repeat— do not discard them! In the Bible, Daniel had a dream, and he wrote down the *substance* of it (Daniel 7:1). Different translations call it the main facts, a summary, or the sum of the matters. Basically, Daniel took what he was able to get without remembering every detail. Personally, reading that was *super* encouraging to me and hopefully to you as well. Just remember that there's grace and record your dreams first upon waking.

Lastly, I do want to mention that some details are not essential to note in the grand scheme of things. While helping others interpret dreams, I usually ask them detailed questions to get a better understanding of the dream. I've learned if the dreamer doesn't remember specific details like the color of clothes, the features of a face, or the awareness of the surroundings, then it most likely isn't crucial to the overall plot of the dream (we will learn more about the details of dreams in the next section).

All in all, don't beat yourself up if you are having difficulties remembering your dreams. Just continue to steward over your gift of dreaming and apply the practical steps to glean as much information as you can.

Part Two | How to Crack the Dream Code

Introduction

So, we've finally made it past part one! *Yay! Clap for yourself!* In this part, we will discuss *how* to crack the dream code. You may be wondering why I decided to speak about this next instead of going straight into symbols. Since I'm going to repeat this over and over again (brace yourself), I might as well say it here too. The biggest secret to cracking the dream code is... *come closer...* the technique. *Shhh!* It's our little secret. Too many dream coders get *sooo* stuck on the symbols that they miss context and what God is trying to say (don't let that be you).

From my experience, God dreams need the most technique and understanding. Usually, overtly demonic dreams and soul dreams are relatively quick and to the point. I personally have not experienced in my time decoding dreams a demonic dream that was long and elaborate. Any scary, intricate dream is usually a warning or correctional dream from God.

I believe this is so because demons can only imitate; they cannot create. God is the Creator of the whole universe and everything in it. Demons can only copy (very poorly at that) what they see the Creator do. They usually don't put that much effort and don't pay attention to details in dreams.

I say all that to say this section will be mostly about how to decode dreams from God. Without further ado, let's get into it!

The Methodology

I wish I could tell you a pivotal point in time when everything just clicked, and this methodology was born. I guess it was a combination of the Holy Spirit, a lot of practice, and exposure to different types of dreams through friends and viewers. Since I was given a strong teaching gift, I was able to explain to others the step-by-step approach I use to interpret dreams.

I call this technique the *Fold, Organize, and Put Away Method*. If we were to think of our dreams as clean laundry, folding would involve decoding the symbols, organizing would involve finding the interpretation, and putting it away would involve understanding the application.

If we were to think of our dreams as clean laundry, the first thing you would do is grab and pick out the crumpled and wrinkled information from your dream, straighten it out and fold it by decoding the symbols you have seen. In the same way that you would take a folded T-shirt and organize it into a stack with other T-shirts, or separate and distinguish your husband's clothes from your own, you would organize the information from your dream into an interpretation. Lastly, you would take those organized (interpreted dreams) clothes and put it away in the drawers of your life to which they belong. Putting away means understanding the application of what you have interpreted to the appropriate areas of your life.

I won't lie; this method is a bit tedious. But this is the most thorough and beginner-friendly method I have used when it comes to interpreting dreams.

So, I know I teased you a bit by telling you about the methodology we're going to explore, but there is *sooo* much we have to unpack before we're able to confidently crack the dream code.

Different Levels of Dreams

Before we begin interpreting dreams, it may be helpful to understand the different levels of dreams and how to approach them.

Literal Dreams

Let's talk about literal dreams first. Although we spoke about these types of dreams earlier, I think it's important to know how to approach them when we recognize them.

To recap, literal dreams do not have any symbolism and are straight to the point. These types of dreams are usually easy to spot because there's no funny business going on. There's nothing to decode, and usually, the dreamer can immediately apply what they've received from the dream. For the most part, some instructional dreams fall into this category.

Simple Dreams

Simple dreams are dreams with minimal symbols and scenes. These types of dreams usually are one to two scenes and have a small number of details. When I host live dream interpretation Q&As on YouTube, I decode simple dreams for others. If you can fit your dream within 500 characters, then it's probably a simple dream.

Complex Dreams

Complex dreams involve multiple scenes and are super detailed. These types of dreams are the ones a dreamer really has to sit down and take his or her time with. For the most part, these dreams have a lot to unpack and the meaning is deeply hidden from the dreamer.

Multi-Layered Dreams

Multi-Layered dreams are dreams with more than one meaning or a deeper meaning. You're probably wondering, *Aren't most dreams multi-layered because they involve symbolism?* Well to an extent, yes. But multi-layered symbols involve multiple meanings. Have you ever heard of double entendres? Yeah. That's how I would describe a multi-layered dream.

So, there's no specific example of a multi-layered *dream* in the Bible, but there was a multi-layered *sign* we can discuss.

Let's look into Daniel 5. Before we pick apart the text, I want to give you some background information. So there was a King named Belshazzar of Babylon, and he threw a great banquet. For his banquet, he used some sacred objects from the temple of Jerusalem (already off to a bad start, buddy). While they were partying, a human hand wrote a cryptic message on the wall. King Belshazzar was so afraid and asked all the wise men of Babylon to interpret the meaning, but they could not. Eventually, they summoned

Daniel, who was an Israelite, to interpret the message. Let's take a look.

Daniel 5:25 New International Version (NIV)

25 "This is the inscription that was written:

mene, mene, tekel, parsin

Now let's break it down:

- **Mene**: This stands for *mina* which is a unit of money or *numbered*.
- **Tekel**: This stands for *shekel* which was determined by *weight*.
- **Peres**: This is the singular of *Parsin* which means *divided*, the kingdom of *Persia*, or *half* of a mina or shekel

So, if we were to break this down literally it's saying, "number, number, weigh, divide." *Huh?* Exactly. This is why no one knew what it meant not because they didn't speak Aramaic, which was the national language, but to the unassuming person, it looks like gibberish. It's important to notice that this is a multi-layered message. We got what it means at the surface level, but let's see what Daniel has to say about it.

26 "Here is what these words mean:

Mene[e]: God has numbered the days of your reign and brought it to an end.

27 Tekel[f]: You have been weighed on the scales and found wanting.

28 Peres[g]: Your kingdom is divided and given to the Medes and Persians."

Yikes! This was not a good message at all. As we can see, that message was a coming prophecy about King Belshazzar. We find out in the next few verses that the king was assassinated. *Whew! God don't playyy!*

I'll give another example of a multi-layered symbol I received. I mentioned earlier that a young lady had an encouragement dream, and in it, she had a high credit score. Well, there was a lot more to the dream, and a huge part was how *specific* her score was. Her credit score in the dream was 679. *Hmmm...* It seemed like a significant detail, so I pressed in. Then all of a sudden, Holy Spirit dropped the revelation on me! Each number was significant and revealed a bigger picture of what was going on in this young lady's life.

Firstly, I thought it was interesting that the normal progression of numbers would be 6,7, and then 8, but this sequence skipped 8. Although we'll discuss biblical numerology in the Appendix, the number 8 represents new beginnings and the number 9 represents fruitfulness or fullness.

So, the interpretation that was given to me was this:

- This young lady has a lot of integrity which was symbolized by her high credit score.
- Because of her high integrity, something that should've been a new start will reach its maturity quickly.
- Something new is going to happen in this young lady's life but will seem like the equivalent of a woman giving birth to a full-grown human!

Wow! Even up to this day, your girl is still shook. I couldn't believe how God used that multi-layered symbol and intertwined it through the message of the dream. He is so creative! All in all, multi-layered dreams involve more than meets the eye.

Different Types of Dreamers

Now we understand the different levels of dreams, let's discuss the different levels of dream interpretation. This is so important to know and understand so that you can get a sense of where you are and what you personally can improve on. Sometimes we beat ourselves up because we are comparing the way we interpret dreams to everyone else and have certain unrealistic expectations towards cracking the dream code. Listen, my dear, you are in a lane of your own. Everyone is at a different point in their journey, so don't compare your stage one to someone's stage ten. *Hey! That'll preach!*

Novice Dreamers

A novice dreamer is a dreamer who dreams but has no idea what they mean. I mean like none. They probably know that there is something more to this dream thing, but they have difficulties interpreting their own dreams.

Raise your hand if you're in this camp! I bet a lot of us are. If this is you, well I'm glad you're here! You've definitely come to the right place. The biggest things to grasp at this phase are understanding how God speaks to you and symbolism. We will go over how to grow in these two areas in the next sections, but this is the crux of how to crack the code.

Intermediate Dreamers

Now let's move on to intermediate dreamers. These people can usually make some sense of their dreams but may have difficulties interpreting intricate dreams and other people's dreams. Usually, dreamers at this stage have mastered symbolism or the way God speaks to them. I've noticed intermediate dreamers have difficulties growing in interpretation because they have not found a harmonious balance between decoding symbols and yielding to the voice of God. Also, at this level, it's important to master simple dreams.

Advanced Dreamers

Lastly, there are those who are advanced dreamers. These dreamers have mastered symbolism and the way God speaks to them. They are usually able to interpret their own dreams and others. At this level, they have achieved decoding simple dreams, complex dreams, and multi-layered symbols.

Everyone compares themselves to this level, but the truth is, most dreamers are novice dreamers. This is why you can't beat yourself up for not knowing how to decode your dreams! *Like, you good.* Just keep practicing and learning. Remember, Rome wasn't built in a day!

Now let's discuss how God speaks to us and symbolism.

How God Speaks to You

If I could be honest with you, it grieves me how ill-equipped the modern-day Church is. A lot of us have been fooled into thinking that only our pastors or spiritual leaders hear from God and have all the answers. Please understand that I believe in spiritual authority and having godly counsel. Still, my gripe is when people don't have the tools or the understanding to encounter God on a day-to-day basis in their individual walk.

In this section, I will share with you the common ways God communicates to us individually. Although this section will be helpful for your Christian walk in general, it will also help you in dream interpretation. Earlier we mentioned that two things novice and intermediate dreamers must master are symbolism and the way God speaks to them. We'll learn about symbolism in a bit, but now we have to dissect the different ways God communicates to us.

This concept is very important to grasp because dream interpretation is not strictly about knowing what symbols mean and memorizing dream dictionaries. *Listennn* to the Holy Spirit. Go with your hunch when decoding dreams even if you're not completely certain about the symbols. Have the confidence that if you are a born-again Christian, then the Holy Spirit resides in you. Be aware of your relationship with God and how He communicates with you so that you can grow in dream interpretation.

Now before we continue into the different ways God communicates with us, I do want to note that God speaks to us primarily through His Word and His Spirit. But even when He speaks to us personally, it will NEVER contradict His Word. If it does contradict God's Word, then we have to assume the message was not from God.

For example, if a young lady believes that God told her that a currently married man will be her husband, then we as believers could judge righteously and say that wasn't God speaking. *Don't be that person, sis (or bro).* Be sure to measure any messages you think you receive from God up against the standard of the Word of God.

I've noticed that many people have received revelations from God, but they have a lot of self-doubt and wonder if it really is God speaking to them. Maybe you have questioned how to determine if it's God communicating to you, the enemy, or just you. Like I just mentioned, God will never contradict His Word or character. God's word is life-giving, challenges us to do better, and is true. There are so many more attributes we could discuss, but I think it's just important to study the Word of God and spend intimate time with Him.

As far as the different ways God speaks to us individually, most of us have a primary way that God communicates to us, and sometimes, a secondary way as well. I believe it is essential to understand the way God speaks to *you* so that you can be able to interpret your dreams better. When you have clarity of this, it may give you more confidence discerning your dreams.

Feeling

One way God can speak to us is through feeling. Feelers usually use phrases like, "I feel like God is telling me this," or "Something feels off." Feelers connect with God through their emotions and physical senses.

Some scenarios that describe feelers:

- Feeling dizzy or having headaches in an atmosphere with a lot of spiritual warfare
- Crying in the presence of God
- Feeling troubled around certain people or places
- Physical sensations in the body

Knowing

Some people call it intuition, but knowers communicate to God directly through an assuredness in their spirit. Knowing is a difficult concept to understand for most people, especially to those who are knowers themselves. Because there is no direct evidence of knowing, most knowers don't even realize this is a way God speaks to them. A friend of mine has said that knowing requires a lot of faith, which I agree with.

Some examples that classify knowers:

- Having an unexplainable "gut feeling" about something
- Tension or resistance in the spirit to do or not do something or to say or not say something
- Strong faith

Seeing

Seers, or people who have a gift of seeing, interact with God visually. The seeing realm is a realm of the spirit that constitutes visions, dreams, and brief images. Although dreaming is part of the seeing realm, seers also experience visions and pictures while they are awake. The Holy Spirit will imprint specific images into the mind of a seer, or they may experience visions in waking life. This mode of communication is another tricky one for people to understand because many people who have a gift of seeing may think they're crazy or are hallucinating. This explanation is not to downplay those who do need medical help, but some seers might feel stigmatized for some things that they see.

Some experiences of seers:

- Seeing picture riddles (for example, they may be talking to a person then see an image of them climbing a mountain)
- Seeing heavenly beings (angels and demons)
- Seeing people's faces flash quickly in their minds

Hearing

Ever have a thought that intersects your own, and you just *knew* it wasn't you? So is the life of hearers. God communicates with hearers through audible stimuli or thoughts spoken in their minds. Similarly, with seers, hearers can often be stigmatized and think what they're hearing is delusional. Again, this is not to be mistaken for people who actually need medical attention, but hearing is a way that God speaks to some of us.

Some hearers may experience:

- Sound riddles (for example, hearing a knock when no one is knocking or hearing the sound of rushing waters)
- Hearing the audible voice of God (extremely rare and not common)
- Hearing thoughts in your mind that you know is not your own

Understanding Symbolism

So let's discuss symbolism! *Woo boy!* Depending on the person, symbolism can be easy or difficult to grasp. If you're someone like me who is very logical, practical, and concrete, then mastering symbolism may be challenging. If you are more right-brained, creative, artsy, and abstract, then it may be easy for you to master this concept.

When it comes to symbolism, the biggest thing to realize is that it's not about the symbols themselves. It's about *training your mind* to understand symbolism. Let me give you an analogy. If you've ever taken a college entry exam in the United States, then you know there are two sets of tests to take—the SAT and the ACT. The ACT is more knowledge-based and about what you learned in high school. The SAT, on the other hand, is not really about what you know. It's about *how* you think. There are certain techniques taught to master the SAT and pass. If you take the SAT and simply study the questions, you more than likely wouldn't do so hot or even complete the exam in time. Same with cracking the dream code! Repeat after me—*it is not only about the symbols or memorization. It is not only about symbols or memorization. It is not only about symbols or memorization.* Got it? Good!

So how do we train our minds to understand symbolism? Quoting Rafiki the baboon in the Lion King 1 ½, "Look beyond what you see." If we understand that dreams are usually symbolic, let's think of what they could mean past the literal images we're given. Let's go over some basic everyday objects and walk through the process of discovering the symbolism for each one.

Plant

So, let's say you see a plant. Besides it being a plant, what does your mind think of when you think of a basic, ordinary plant? Go ahead, think about it… Did you think about it? Awesome! If you're like most people, maybe growth or natural comes to mind first (unless you're a genius and you thought of something else). Therefore, a plant can *symbolize* growth. Wasn't that easy? And you didn't need a dream symbol dictionary either!

Crown

What comes to mind when you think of a crown? *Don't overthink it either!* Most people would think of royalty, authority, or kingship when they think of a crown. They may connect it to who wears the crown (which would be a king, queen, etc.) and what the person wearing the crown does. Hence why a crown could *represent* royalty, authority, or kingship. *You're doin' amazing, sweetie!*

Book

Lastly, let's talk about a book. Everyone reads books. What do you think of when you think of books? Probably reading, learning, or information, right? If that's the case, then a book can represent learning something or gaining information. *You see? You got this! High five!*

As we can see, symbolism is very possible to master. Personally, for me, since I'm very analytical and logical, symbolism for me was difficult to understand at first. When I was in school, I would always do better in math than reading because math was concrete. I liked following formulas and the assuredness that one plus one would always equal two. Reading and English was a whole different ball game for me, especially when I took advanced placement courses in high school. I absolutely hated dissecting poetry and reading artistic literature because symbolism made no sense to me. I feel like this changed, though, after I got saved and became a disciple of Christ. Since the Bible in one-third poetry and I grew to enjoy reading it, symbolism became an easier concept to grasp. Little by little, metaphors, similes, parables, and other literary devices began to make sense and help me with dream interpretation. Hopefully, my mini testimony encouraged you!

Let's move on to understanding symbols on a deeper level within dream interpretation.

The Different Categories of Symbols

Most symbols can fall into one of four categories: general, personal, biblical, and cultural. It's helpful to know this because many people who rely heavily on dream symbol dictionaries (that is, references that decode dream symbols) don't realize that some decoded symbols do not apply to their life and the context of their dreams. Once you understand the different symbol categories, it will be easier for you to master dream interpretation.

General Symbols

As mentioned earlier, some symbols are straightforward or universal. For example, if you see a key in a dream, it doesn't matter who the dreamer is or what culture he or she is from, keys open something or give access to something. That would be the symbolism of a key and therefore it is a general/universal symbol.

Although that was a straightforward example, there are some general symbols that a person would only know if they have a background in dream interpretation. Some cases would be houses, automobiles, teeth, food, etc. We will get into these symbols and their meanings in part three and the appendix.

Personal Symbols

So let's discuss personal symbols. These are symbols that the dreamer has a personal connection with. For example, a friend or coworker can be a personal symbol. Also, TV shows, movies, and celebrities are personal symbols.

I believe people have the tendencies to throw away dreams with many personal symbols because they believe they are soul dreams. I think many dreamers gravitate to this possibility because they lack the understanding that God is personal, speaks our language, and understands our culture.

Firstly, it is vital to recognize that the Judeo-Christian God is a personal, intimate God. Our God is not distant and aloof to who we are. He sees us and knows us by name. He knows our thoughts and what we're going to say even before we say it (It sounds creepy, but it's so cool. I promise). When you understand your identity as a child of God, it is easy to see that God wants to be involved in every area of our lives. Since God wants intimate relationships with His children, it's clear to see why He would use symbols that you would identify within your dreams.

The next concept to grasp as to why God uses personal symbols is because He speaks our language and knows our culture. Have you ever thought of that? God knows every single language on earth and every culture there ever was. Most of us know that unconsciously but have not connected it with how He communicates with us. As I said before, God is not in the business of tricking us, and He is not the author of confusion. God uses imagery and representations in the dreamer's language and culture because *He's* trying to communicate with *the dreamer*! Still not fully convinced that the Lord would speak to you using a reality tv show or pop culture reference? Well, look in the Bible. There were so many things God said that to us may seem a bit strange, but to the ancient Israelites, it made complete sense. Even Jesus Himself used parables that described the culture of His time. Jesus understood His audience and knew how to relate to them. So does God in our dreams!

All in all, this category is probably one of the biggest reasons why I believe it is unwise to rely heavily on dream dictionaries. You have to remember that *you* are the one who received the dream, so *you* are the best person to interpret it. This reason is why when I coach people or interpret dreams, I always ask, *what does this symbol mean to YOU*? If you see someone wearing polka dots in a dream and you have a deep fear of that pattern, how is anyone supposed to know that? If you are a vet or have a pet dog, the meaning of a dog in a dream will most likely be completely different compared to someone who is neutral or fearful of dogs. This reason is why when you sit down to decode your symbols, the first question you should ask yourself is, *what is the symbolism?* Then, *what does this symbol mean to me?*

Biblical Symbols

Biblical symbols are symbols referenced in the Bible. Since God gives us dreams sometimes, it would only make sense that His written Word would validate a dream. There have been so many dreams I have helped interpret that were literally bible scriptures embedded into the dream. For this reason, if you want to sharpen your gift of interpretation, you must be a student of the Word of God. You would be surprised at how many common dream symbols are, in fact, biblical. Some examples include houses, colors, numbers, characters, and objects. It would benefit you when you get stuck on a symbol, simply ask the Holy Spirit, then research if that particular symbol is in the Bible and what the Bible has to say about it.

Cultural Symbols

The last category on our list of symbols is cultural symbols. Culture plays a huge part in the way we relate to the world around us and, ultimately, how we dream. Let's take hand signs, for example. In the United States, a thumbs-up means good job, confirmation, or affirmation. But in countries such as Afghanistan, Iran, and parts of Italy and Greece, it means something vulgar. Let's take another example that is more timebound. In the twenty-first century and in the Western world, phones, the internet, and social media are huge parts of everyday life and culture. Someone, on the other hand, who lived hundreds of years ago may have more experiences on a farm. This is the reason why the Bible does not hold every symbol because the Bible was written by a certain group of people in a bound time period and in a particular culture. So, depending on the dreamer, what culture they grew up in, and what time period they lived in, different symbols could have different implications.

Perfectionism vs Grace

The next thing we have to discuss is how to break perfectionism. I believe perfectionism is just a combination of pride and fear. It's pride because we are depending on ourselves when we need to depend on God. Whether that is performance, intellect, or work, we tend to lean on our own strength. Perfectionism is also fear because we become fearful of the unknown and what will happen if we get something wrong. Honestly, this is probably the biggest hindrance in learning how to interpret dreams, and it is so frustrating!

Perfectionism can be developed through soul wounds (that is, wounds that affect our thoughts, emotions, and intellect) inflicted by others, especially our families. Whether we've had parents who were absent, unreliable, strict, or overly critical, it can breed seeds of perfectionism and ultimately affect our relationship with God. When we see God as a slave driver, a harsh ruler, or a distant God, we will be more afraid to make mistakes. Fortunately, God is nothing like our earthly parents or rulers. He is loving, patient, caring, and gentle. If you want to grow in dream interpretation, you must renew your mind on the way you view God. There is grace, and you don't have to be afraid to make a mistake. God is not trying to trick you, and He is not going to punish you if you don't understand something. We must realize that it is God's desire for us to receive revelation and to communicate with Him. He's not sitting there waiting for you to fail just to jump up and point out all your mistakes. Please get that image out of your mind.

It's so important to truly be aware and overcome perfectionism because that will be the biggest thing to hold you back in the realm of dream interpretation. Listen, friend. There is no perfectionism with God. Just do your best, and God will do the rest. Remember what type of dreamer you are, and don't compare yourself either. No one has more of God and His grace than you do. As we'll discover shortly, we are not the ones who hold the interpretation of dreams—God is. Our strength and ability to interpret come from God and not ourselves.

Maybe Faith

Pastor Mike Todd once preached a series of talks called *Crazy Faith*. In one part, he preached a sermon entitled *Maybe Faith*, and in it, he explained that if we are at least 51% sure of something God had spoken, then we now have "maybe faith." This teaching has been instrumental in my experience coaching others on how to interpret dreams. When I see my students get stuck or are struggling with perfectionism, I ask them to tap into their maybe faith. I found that many people have an idea of what a symbol means, but because they are afraid or do not understand the way God speaks to them, they end up keeping silent. Too many people think that they have to be one hundred percent certain of what something means, but dream interpretation doesn't work like that. You may never feel one hundred percent sure if what you assumed is correct, which is okay!

Please drill this point into your mind: If you have any ounce of "maybe faith," just go with it and see where it leads you. A quote I heard in a movie called *A Cinderella Story* was "never let the fear of striking out keep you from playing the game." You got this, and God got you! If you are a born-again believer with the Holy Spirit dwelling inside of you, then trust that He is working, even if you don't feel completely confident.

The Holy Spirit

So, we're almost done and at the technique! But before we get there, there is an important pre-step we have to acquire if we want a more profound revelation of dreams. Before we even touch a dream and start decoding, we must obtain the help of the Holy Spirit.

As believers who are born again, we all have the Holy Spirit dwelling within each of us, and part of the function of the Holy Spirit is to distribute spiritual gifts (1 Cor 12:11). Although not specified as one of the manifestation gifts of the Spirit in 1 Corinthians 12, the ability to interpret dreams is a gift in and of itself. We can invite the power of the Holy Spirit to help us unlock this gift.

Let's take a look at the life of Joseph, the dreamer, in Genesis 37. Joseph had two dreams that he told his family, and they were able to interpret it instantly. Although the

Bible does not record the motive behind why Joseph told his family his dreams, it is quite possible that Joseph himself did not know the meaning of the dreams and did not yet possess the gift of dream interpretation. His family had the natural ability to interpret dreams, but perhaps Joseph had to grow and mature in that gift.

Skipping ahead to chapter 40, we see Joseph has been through some hardships and now is in jail. A baker and a cupbearer were also thrown into prison and have had dreams but no one to interpret it for them. It is then that Joseph makes a profound statement and says that all interpretations belong to God (Gen 40:8).

This is the reason why before you interpret a dream, you must invite the Holy Spirit *because He is the one who holds the interpretation*. Although the Holy Spirit is always with us, praying and inviting Him in makes us more aware of His presence and helps us yield to whatever God would like to reveal for us. When we jump straight into interpreting dreams, our perfectionism may creep up because we assume that we are the ones who hold the understanding. We may end up becoming fearful and give up altogether, which is why it's essential to lean on God when interpreting dreams.

Folding (Decoding Symbols)

Yay! We've finally renewed and prepared our minds to interpret dreams. I know you probably wanted to jump straight into the technique but trust me. You'll thank me later.

The first and most significant step in this methodology is to fold (decode symbols). This step trips people up the most because the question is always *what if I don't know what the symbol means?* Contrary to popular belief, interpreting dreams is not as mystical as it seems to be.

In this step, all you must do is go through each detail of the dream and decode the symbol. Think about what each symbol means in real life and what each symbol means to you. Although we will go more in-depth about some symbols in part three and the appendix, we can still practice basic interpretation with what we've learned.

Surprisingly in the Bible, Joseph, the dreamer, used this same method to decode Pharaoh's dream. Although he didn't call it the Fold, Organize, and Put Away Method, the concept is still the same. Let's take a look at Pharaoh's dream in Genesis 41:17-27:

17 Then Pharaoh said to Joseph, "In my dream I was standing on the bank of the Nile, 18 when out of the river there came up seven cows, fat and sleek, and they grazed among the reeds. 19 After them, seven other cows came up—scrawny and very ugly and lean. I had never seen such ugly cows in all the land of Egypt. 20 The lean, ugly cows ate up the seven fat cows that came up first. 21 But even after they ate them, no one could tell that they had done so; they looked just as ugly as before. Then I woke up.

22 "In my dream I saw seven heads of grain, full and good, growing on a single stalk. 23 After them, seven other heads sprouted—withered and thin and scorched by the east wind. 24 The thin heads of grain swallowed up the seven good heads.

Now let's see how Joseph folds:

25 Then Joseph said to Pharaoh, "The dreams of Pharaoh are one and the same. God has revealed to Pharaoh what he is about to do. 26 The seven good cows are seven years, and the seven good heads of grain are seven years; it is one and the same dream. 27 The seven lean, ugly cows that came up afterward are seven years, and so are the seven worthless heads of grain scorched by the east wind: They are seven years of famine.

- **The seven good cows**: seven years
- **The seven good heads of grain**: seven years
- **The seven lean, ugly cows**: seven years of famine
- **Seven worthless heads of grain**: seven years of famine

It seems almost too easy, but I have seen many people I coach fumble on this step time after time. To further your understanding of how to fold, I will give you some tips to help make it more practical. After that, I will go into the common mistakes I see people make at the folding stage.

Tip #1: Think About What the Symbol Means in Real Life

As I said, dreams and symbols are not as mysterious as we may have thought initially. Although some symbols require a bit more thought or previous experience with dream interpretation, I would say over half of all the symbols that you dream directly relates to the function it has in real life. For example, let's take a mirror. If you were to see a mirror in a dream, what would you think it means? If we think about the function of a mirror in real life, it will correlate in the dream. A mirror shows us our reflection, allows us to see our flaws, and allows us to check ourselves. So, if we were to see a mirror in a dream, it would represent self-examination of ourselves, heart, and motives. Although there are nuances depending on the context of the dream, that is a good place to start.

Tip #2: Come Back to Ambiguous Symbols

So, remember when I said that over half of all symbols are pretty straightforward? Well, the rest is sometimes not as easy to decode. This realization is especially true when it comes to characters and sometimes objects or events in dreams, which we will discuss later. From my experience, when you see a character in a dream, it's only a literal symbol maybe a quarter of the time. The majority of the time you see people in a dream, they are symbolic of something else. So, if you are folding and are unsure of what a particular character, object, or event represents, don't stay stuck on it. Come back to it when it's time to organize, and you have more context. You may be surprised when you discover that symbol represents a spirit, you, God, your past, or a representation of something else.

Tip #3: Don't Overcomplicate A Symbol

Dreams are already confusing in and of itself, but sometimes we unknowingly overcomplicate things. What I see happen at times is that people don't trust the Holy Spirit and themselves, so they try to pick apart a symbol. Let's say, for example, someone has a dream that they are running through a forest. Some people may freak out because they don't understand the symbolism of a forest. What ends up happening is that the person will begin to dissect the whole forest to trees, leaves, dirt, sky, and atoms (I'm joking, but this is a real thing)! If this is you, just take a deep breath and remember the Holy Spirit is with you. Instead of looking too deeply into a symbol, try to look at symbols through the context of the dream. I know some of us are super spiro (spiritual), but it ain't that deep. Guard yourself against the urge to overcomplicate symbols and trust your intuition.

Tip #4: Remember the Holy Spirit

Although we discussed the Holy Spirit as a pre-step to interpreting dreams, I just want to remind you to utilize Him while you fold. Sometimes when I coach people, they reach a symbol that they don't understand, and they become crippled with fear and anxiety. Just… relax. This is not a test nor something that you have to do alone. We must let go of perfectionism and remember that the Holy Spirit is a gentleman who will not force Himself on us. You must invite Him in and let Him sit in the driver's seat, not fear. Please understand that God is not going to punish you because you don't know what a symbol means, so just relax and simply ask, *Holy Spirit, what does this mean*?

Now that we have discussed different tips to help you decode your symbols, let's discuss the common mistakes people usually make while they are still in the folding stage.

Mistake #1: Organizing and Putting Away While You are Still Folding

If this isn't the biggest mistake I've seen throughout dream coaching, then I don't know what is. While decoding symbols, often the dreamer will decode one or two symbols, it resonates with them, then he or she will try to jump ahead to the interpretation, or what God is trying to tell him or her. THIS IS A MISTAKE. Although it seems reasonable, I always make the analogy that you can't tell what a movie is about based on the trailer. The purpose of folding is to simply decode the symbols. I know you want to jump straight into the meaning, but it will benefit you the most to do this orderly.

I also want to mention that symbols usually don't make sense at this step, and that's okay! If I were to give another analogy, I'd say interpreting dreams is like translating a language. We cannot know the whole meaning of a passage by just translating one word. I want to reiterate that all we are doing at this step is *just folding*. Resist the temptation to gain an understanding of the dream at this point and keep folding.

Mistake #2: Skipping Small but Important Details

If you're new to dream interpretation or have just begun to shift your mindset on how you view dreams, then this mistake is understandable. Many times, when people don't understand the complexities of dreams, they tend to skip over details that are, in fact, very integral to the plot of the dream. For example, a friend had a dream, and in it, she passed by a white washer and dryer. Initially, she didn't think much of it and almost didn't mention it because she didn't interact with it. Also, it seemed completely random. Apparently, it had some significance to the overall message of the dream. *Who knew?* Or how about a dreamer who saw a man wearing all red pass her by in a dream? This is something that could easily be passed up as random or meaningless. But all these scenarios are examples of how small, insignificant things should be taken into account when it comes to dreams.

Dreams are like movies; details never are wasted. How many times have you watched a movie, and the seemingly irrelevant information ended up being essential to the climax? Probably many times. I'm always surprised at how a film can use the mundane and tie it into the plot. For this reason, while folding your dreams, don't forget to decode the perceived unimportant details.

Mistake #3: Forcing Meaning onto A Symbol

This is a mistake most wouldn't regularly catch unless they are seasoned in dream interpretation. This mistake ties into Mistake #1, and sometimes we can get in our own way. Often, we decode two symbols and have a hint on what the dream *could* be about, and then we try to quickly force the rest of the symbols to support our assumption. THIS IS A MISTAKE. Although I don't doubt that your hypothesis could be right, do not try to force a square peg into a round hole. If you're new to interpreting dreams, I would say to keep an open mind. You don't want to confuse yourself while you're folding, so focus on just decoding the symbols.

Mistake #4: Jumping Straight to the Climax

Look, I get it. You had a dream where you were naked, pregnant, defecating, etc. I get it. Dreams are wild, but you cannot just jump straight into the climax of a dream. So much happened before and after that point that was probably symbolic as well. Again, we cannot judge a movie by its trailer, nor can we judge a book by its cover. What I see happen a lot when I'm coaching people is that while we're folding, instead of taking each symbol piece by piece, they run ahead and rush to the climax. Yes, there may be a general theme, but it is so important to not focus on the dream as if it is reality. What I mean is that many people will be so caught up by the dream itself but not focused enough on the symbolism behind it. Let's say if someone has a dream that pregnancy is the central theme, they will be so focused on that detail and disregard the rest of the dream and the symbolism behind it.

When it comes to folding, it is so important to take apart the dream piece by piece. Jumping straight into the climax is equivalent to having a mountain of clean laundry, and instead of taking an article of clothing from the top of the pile, you pull straight from the middle. Guess what happens when you do that? You've guessed right. The whole pile of clothes topples over.

Organizing (Interpretation)

I know we spent a lot of time on folding, but I believe folding is the most important foundational step. The next step we're going to talk about is organizing (interpretation). If we revisit the analogy about translating languages, interpreting would be stringing the translated words into a comprehensive sentence. At this stage, we're giving context and meaning to the decoded symbols.

Let's revisit Pharaoh's dreams and see how Joseph organizes it.

Genesis 41

17 Then Pharaoh said to Joseph, "In my dream I was standing on the bank of the Nile, 18 when out of the river there came up seven cows, fat and sleek, and they grazed among the reeds. 19 After them, seven other cows came up—scrawny and very ugly and lean. I had never seen such ugly cows in all the land of Egypt. 20 The lean, ugly cows ate up the seven fat cows that came up first. 21 But even after they ate them, no one could tell that they had done so; they looked just as ugly as before. Then I woke up.

22 "In my dream I saw seven heads of grain, full and good, growing on a single stalk. 23 After them, seven other heads sprouted—withered and thin and scorched by the east wind. 24 The thin heads of grain swallowed up the seven good heads.

Fold

25 Then Joseph said to Pharaoh, "The dreams of Pharaoh are one and the same. God has revealed to Pharaoh what he is about to do. 26 The seven good cows are seven years, and the seven good heads of grain are seven years; it is one and the same dream. 27 The seven lean, ugly cows that came up afterward are seven years, and so are the seven worthless heads of grain scorched by the east wind: They are seven years of famine.

- **The seven good cows**: seven years
- **The seven good heads of grain**: seven years
- **The seven lean, ugly cows**: seven years of famine
- **Seven worthless heads of grain**: seven years of famine

Organize

28 "It is just as I said to Pharaoh: God has shown Pharaoh what he is about to do. 29 Seven years of great abundance are coming throughout the land of Egypt, 30 but seven years of famine will follow them. Then all the abundance in Egypt will be forgotten, and the famine will ravage the land. 31 The abundance in the land will not be remembered, because the famine that follows it will be so severe. 32 The reason the dream was given to Pharaoh in two forms is that the matter has been firmly decided by God, and God will do it soon.

- Seven years of great abundance are coming throughout the land of Egypt, but seven years of famine will follow them.
- The abundance in the land will not be remembered, because the famine that follows it will be so severe.

Once you have folded, organizing and putting it away becomes easier.

Tip #1: Use Context

Let's keep it real. Some symbols have a LOT of meanings, especially when it comes to characters and colors. This is why it's important to consider the context and how the symbol fits into the entire interpretation to determine what it really meant. You may have thought a symbol meant one thing initially, but in fact, it could mean something completely different! For example, let's say you initially thought a character wearing all red symbolized Jesus Christ, but then that character is doing something sinful. So obviously, that person was not representing Jesus Christ. When you get to the organizing step and have more context of the dream, you might discover that person symbolized rage, anger, or war. We always have to remember that context is key!

In addition to context, I want to stress again that you cannot solely rely on a dream dictionary to interpret your dreams for you. I feel like I'm beating a dead horse when I keep repeating this, but I want you to really understand how limiting dream dictionaries are. Although some good ones will give you positive and negative meanings of a symbol (because they know context is key), most will give you a one-dimensional view on a symbol.

Tip #2: Consider the Flow of the Dream

Although dreams seem very whimsical and random, we must also see them as practical. I'm referring to the flow of a dream. What happened after this detail, and how does it connect with what just happened?

Many dreams are long and complex, while some are short and straight to the point. For longer dreams with multiple scenes, try to organize by scenes. Before the scene and setting changed, what happened? How does everything correlate together? For example, someone shared with me a dream they had where he or she was in a rental property home. This person looked outside, had a beautiful vision, went out, then went back into the same rental home. On the surface, one may just interpret the symbols and keep moving, but there was a particular *flow* to the dream. Most people would have skipped over the fact that the dreamer just went back to a place he or she left. That is significant. If a rental property means a temporary place in one's life, then that would mean the dreamer went back to a season that he or she should've already completed.

Tip #3: Create A Synonym

Sometimes it's not the symbols that trip people up, but it's the seemingly random situations that occur. Whether it be an interjection, interaction, or action, these are usually meaningful as well. In these cases, I would suggest creating a synonym that describes the situation in other words. For example, if someone is arguing or fighting you in a dream, you could create a synonym that someone or something is in *battle* with you. From this synonym, it would be easier to see and understand that this situation could represent a spiritual battle or an internal conflict.

Moreover, this tip is also extremely helpful in deciphering personal symbols. For example, I had a dream that I was on a train eating sweet plantain chips. To anyone else, this might seem irrelevant and even random, but this brand of plantain chips I was eating was the best of the best. They are a luxury to me and are very delicious! If I were to give a synonym of myself eating these plantain chips, I would say *sweet* and *luxurious*. When I go back to organize, I would consider this to represent a *sweet ride* in which I will be *well taken care of* (luxury).

All in all, when you are trying to make sense of the symbols and actions in a dream, put it in other words. It helps to break fixation on a weird dream so that you can see the symbolism behind it. Remember, most dreams are not literal! There are deeper meanings behind what you're seeing.

Putting Away (Application)

Now that our laundry has been folded and organized, it's time to put it away. In practical terms, now we have the interpretation, what area of our lives is this dream about, what actions should one take next, and who should one share this information with?

Let's revisit Pharaoh's dream for the last time and see how Joseph puts everything away:

Genesis 41

17 Then Pharaoh said to Joseph, "In my dream I was standing on the bank of the Nile, 18 when out of the river there came up seven cows, fat and sleek, and they grazed among the reeds. 19 After them, seven other cows came up—scrawny and very ugly and lean. I had never seen such ugly cows in all the land of Egypt. 20 The lean, ugly cows ate up the seven fat cows that came up first. 21 But even after they ate them, no one could tell that they had done so; they looked just as ugly as before. Then I woke up.

22 "In my dream I saw seven heads of grain, full and good, growing on a single stalk. 23 After them, seven other heads sprouted—withered and thin and scorched by the east wind. 24 The thin heads of grain swallowed up the seven good heads.

Fold

25 Then Joseph said to Pharaoh, "The dreams of Pharaoh are one and the same. God has revealed to Pharaoh what he is about to do. 26 The seven good cows are seven years, and the seven good heads of grain are seven years; it is one and the same dream. 27 The seven lean, ugly cows that came up afterward are seven years, and so are the seven worthless heads of grain scorched by the east wind: They are seven years of famine.

- **The seven good cows**: seven years
- **The seven good heads of grain**: seven years
- **The seven lean, ugly cows**: seven years of famine
- **Seven worthless heads of grain**: seven years of famine

Organize

28 "It is just as I said to Pharaoh: God has shown Pharaoh what he is about to do. 29 Seven years of great abundance are coming throughout the land of Egypt, 30 but seven years of famine will follow them. Then all the abundance in Egypt will be forgotten, and the famine will ravage the land. 31 The abundance in the land will not be remembered, because the famine that follows it will be so severe. 32 The reason the dream was given to Pharaoh in two forms is that the matter has been firmly decided by God, and God will do it soon.

- Seven years of great abundance are coming throughout the land of Egypt, but seven years of famine will follow them.

- The abundance in the land will not be remembered, because the famine that follows it will be so severe.

Put Away

33 "And now let Pharaoh look for a discerning and wise man and put him in charge of the land of Egypt. 34 Let Pharaoh appoint commissioners over the land to take a fifth of the harvest of Egypt during the seven years of abundance. 35 They should collect all the food of these good years that are coming and store up the grain under the authority of Pharaoh, to be kept in the cities for food. 36 This food should be held in reserve for the country, to be used during the seven years of famine that will come upon Egypt, so that the country may not be ruined by the famine."

- What type of dream is this?
    - Answer: a prophetic warning dream from God
- What is this dream about?
    - Answer: the economy of Egypt
- Who should Pharaoh tell the dream to?
    - Answer: a discerning and wise man
- What actions should be taken?
    - Answer: Pharaoh should appoint commissioners over the land to take a fifth of the harvest of Egypt during the seven years of abundance. They should collect all the food of these good years that are coming and store up the grain under the authority of

Pharaoh, to be kept in the cities for food. This food should be held in reserve for the country, to be used during the seven years of famine that will come upon Egypt, so that the country may not be ruined by the famine.

Listen… Joseph was *that guy*! He really made dream interpretation look like a work of art! Can we just celebrate him for a moment because *sheesh*!

Anyways, let's continue. First, we have to tackle the elephant in the room— what area of the dreamer's life is a dream referring to? Well, I have good news and bad news, so let's start with the bad news. The bad news is that there is no formula to exactly pinpoint what a dream could be referencing. Unlike this systematic method of dream interpretation I'm teaching you, there's not one specific way to cling to when discovering the application. Only the dreamer can fully know what the dream is referencing, and many times you may wind up with more questions than answers after organizing. Think about it like this. You may have a routine way of folding and organizing your laundry, but when it's time to put away clothes, you may put them away in different places. Some clothes may go in the closet. Some go in drawers. And some may need to be hung up. Even if someone was helping you fold and organize your laundry, only *you* know exactly where they're supposed to be put away.

So that was the bad news. The good news is that there are still ways to figure out what area of your life the dream is referencing.

Tip #1: Consider the Personal Symbols

First, the contents of the dream and personal symbols are a huge indicator of what the dream may be referencing. For example, dreaming of being in a childhood home could represent the past and previous experiences. Or let's say your dream involves someone who attends your church, but you may not be close to them. The dream could be about your church. Since there are *sooo* many personal symbols and types of them, there's no way I could exhaust them all. Just be aware of those personal symbols within your dream because they could be a huge clue to what the dream is insinuating.

Tip #2: Consider Your Spiritual Walk

The next way to discover what your dream is implying is to consider your spiritual walk. Since dreams are a form of communication between us and God, it could be helpful to examine your faith walk. For example, let's say you were recently praying about a job opportunity to God. It should come as no surprise that the Lord may answer us that same night through our dreams. Remember, God dreams and Christian dream interpretations should draw us *closer* in relationship with God. For this reason, recalling recent events and experiences with God could help you to understand the application of your dreams. What were you just praying about? What lesson is God currently teaching you? What Scriptures have you just read? Take note of all these questions when you are putting away your dream.

Tip #3: Recognize Themes

Another way to uncover what area of your life a dream could point to is by recognizing key themes in your dreams. If you noticed, Pharaoh's dreams were very similar. Although there were two different symbols, Joseph recognized them as one of the same (Genesis 41:25). He also mentioned that the themes were repeated because it was a matter firmly decided by God (Genesis 41:32). When it comes to dreams, it's important to pay attention to dreams that are similar in nature, have the same symbols, and seem to correlate with one another.

Furthermore, sometimes themes build upon the same idea and paint a clearer picture. For example, a young lady came to me with three very similar dreams. The key theme in all the dreams was that she would pull a piece of her hair down (I assumed she had curly hair) and would be pleasantly surprised that her hair was a lot longer than she thought. She would try to straighten it to see the full length and then she would wake up. It turns out that these dreams were all representing a calling and anointing she had over her life. Her dreams were revealing that she was coming into the knowledge of the *extent* of her callings. She didn't know God was calling her into a greater purpose for her life, but now, she's looking for resources to fully embrace it. If you run into a situation like this, then similar themes can most likely point to the same thing. You may find more information in one dream than another, and that can help you to understand the area of your life the dream is revealing.

Tip #4: Identify the Type of Dream

The next step to take when we put away is to discover what actions to take next. Fortunately, after organizing, we have a clearer picture of the type of dream we're working with. What's the source of the dream and what type of dream is it? Is it an encouragement dream from God? If it is, then the only action to take is to receive the encouragement and be at peace. Is it a terrifying, correctional dream from God? If it is, then probably some repentance and restitution need to take place. Or is it a covertly demonic dream? If it is, then prayer and spiritual warfare may be needed. In any case, it's okay to wrestle with a dream before making the next move. Again, this is not a test, and God is not trying to trick you; He's trying to help you. If you need more clarity or confidence to take the next step, just pray and talk to your Father. Let Him respond to you in whatever way He wants. He may send you to a certain Bible scripture, you may hear a sermon speaking about your situation, or He may send another brother or sister in Christ to encourage you. Be open to how God may answer you.

Tip #5: Use Discernment

Lastly, who should we tell our dreams to? This step takes a bit of discernment on the end of the dreamer. Not everyone needs to know what God told you in a dream (we learned from our buddy Joseph in Genesis 37). Again, depending on the type of dream and contents will determine who you should tell and *when*. Oh, yes. Everyone always forgets about the *when* and gets too caught up with the *what*. For me, I dream about the people around me all the time. Good dreams as well as rebukes. Whether it's a good or bad dream, I take it up in prayer *first*. If I still feel burdened by it, I chew on it for a couple of days. If I haven't forgotten about it by that time and it still burdens me, then I tell the person through the leading of the Holy Spirit. When I do have a word for someone that I received through a dream, I do my best to tell them in the most gracious way possible, and then leave it up to the person and God to take action.

Furthermore, I want to caution you on revealing a word too soon. Whether it's a dream about yourself or a dream about another person, there is always timing. Don't be in a rush to share everything with everyone, especially before the dream has come to pass. Learn from Joseph and *be discerning*! Grow in intimacy with the Holy Spirit so that you can discern other's heart postures. Does the person you are seeking to share your dream struggle with envy, comparison, or bitterness? If you notice certain traits about this person, then you probably shouldn't share it with that person. Don't stress yourself. *It ain't worth it.* Also, is the person that you wish to share your dream with a helpful or encouraging person? Will they speak life into your situation or bring clarity? If they're not going to offer anything relevant to you, again, don't stress yourself. If it's a God dream, it is okay to keep things private between you and God. Not everything needs to be broadcasted to the open heavens.

Tip #6: Be Patient in Your Understanding

Although this may be the easiest step, sometimes it's not. Many times, you can receive an interpretation of a dream and still be confused about what actions to take next or what God is trying to tell you. That's okay. Sometimes God may conceal a meaning so that you will seek Him (Prov 25:2). There have been times I have helped interpret a dream for someone, and they leave with more questions than they have answers. It doesn't mean the interpretation was wrong, but it means that the person needs to seek God to discover *why* they received that message.

All in all, be patient in your understanding. One of my friends said this very casually to me early in my journey, and it stuck with me ever since. Many times, we want an answer immediately, but sometimes we have to chew on what's in front of us and wrestle with it a bit.

Troubleshooting

So, we've discussed how to interpret dreams, but there will be times you're just having difficulties. Here is some help for common problems you may face.

"How many times do I pray to invite the Holy Spirit in? Just once or before every dream?"

While coaching people, I get asked this question often. Please understand that this is not a religious ritual. I only suggest doing this because one, it breaks perfectionism. When you invite the Holy Spirit into your interpreting before you start, it shifts the focus from you to God. It takes you from the fear of not being able to understand the dream, to the realization that you don't hold the meaning in the first place. Two, it gives you an awareness of God. Again, if God holds the interpretation, wouldn't it be nice to bond with Him while you are decoding your dream? All in all, praying to invite the Holy Spirit is less about religion and more about the relationship.

"I just can't seem to figure out this symbol."

That's okay! There will be times that a particular symbol just doesn't click with you. If it is a universal symbol, I would suggest first research if the symbol is biblical and what the bible says about its meaning. If not, look up the general meaning or significance of that symbol. Lastly, consider whether or not that symbol is unique to your culture or context.

"I just saw this situation in real life. Do I discard it as a soul dream?"

Sometimes dreams mimic situations we just saw in reality, and people may feel tempted to throw them away because they seem soulish or they can't find them in a dream dictionary. Although there is a possibility it could be a soul dream, many times, it won't be. If anything, this is an opportunity to expand your capacity in cracking the code and a challenge to get deeper in your understanding. I want to remind you that God can use literally anything to speak to us, so we have to keep an open mind. If God could use a donkey to speak to Balaam (Num 22:21-39), then He could use a current situation to communicate a message to you. Sometimes we have dreams of a conversation we just had, a video we just watched, or a show we just binged on. Even if the dream ends up being a soul dream, God can still use that to speak to us.

"It's taking me too long to do this."

Well, learning any new skill takes work, and in the beginning, you may have put in more work to get the hang of it. The deeper the revelation, the more we may have to dig. Remember, be patient in your understanding. When we were in school learning new, at times, challenging concepts, we didn't get it all in one go. We continued to practice until we mastered it, and I encourage you to do the same.

"I'm overwhelmed!"

Boy, can I relate to this! Sometimes cracking the code can be mentally and spiritually exhausting, especially if it's a very long and elaborate dream. I would say just take it piece by piece and don't overwork yourself. Come back to the rest later after you've given your mind a break. Again, God doesn't expect you to get everything in one go, especially if you're a beginner. You may have to spread your interpreting sessions out and ponder on it for some time.

"I dream a lot and have a busy schedule. What should I do when I get behind in decoding my dreams?"

Whew! Now this is something that I can totally relate to. Sometimes it can be quite difficult to manage this gift, especially when it becomes time-consuming. I would say to give yourself grace, especially if you are a novice or intermediate dreamer. If you're in that boat, remember to try to master your simple dreams *first*. You don't have to bite off more than you can chew, so just focus on the easier dreams until you get the hang of it. Once you're able to handle shorter dreams, then complex and multilayered dreams will become easier to master. Again, Rome was not built in a day. Even if it takes you some years, no one is judging you. You got it!

Also, I want to share with you a phenomenon that happens to me often when I get behind in decoding my dreams. Sometimes when I'm behind even a week in interpreting my dreams, my dreams begin to slow down, and I get more simple and straightforward dreams. I know that's God's mercy over me, and He doesn't want me to get overwhelmed (He is so awesome, honestly). The crazy thing is that when I finally sit down and decode a dream from a week or so ago, I'm always surprised how the dream is speaking to me about what is *currently* happening. Imagine. If I would've sat down to interpret the dream when I had just received it, I would've been a bit stumped because I would have no idea what area of my life it's referring to. But a week later and it's more relevant now more than ever. What an amazing God we serve! I just wanted to share that to encourage you to take it easy on yourself and always remember your identity as a child of God.

Part Three | The Dream Code

Introduction

We've made it to part three! Woohoo! Hope you're not tired yet because the party is just getting started! In this section, I want to teach you about characters and common experiences in dreams. If there were any symbols that need a great deal of elaboration, it would be these two categories. With the information we've gleaned from parts one and two and in addition to part three, you will have the basic tools to interpret most simple dreams and grow in dream interpretation. Use this part as a guide to understand how to interpret characters in dreams as well as common experiences. All other symbols and their meanings will be found in the Appendix. Onward!

Characters

Chances are if you ever had a dream, then you usually are not the only person within it. In this next section, we will discuss characters in dreams. Most characters in dreams fall into one of six categories/representations: yourself, God, angels, demons, the actual person, and a symbol.

A Character Representing Yourself

You probably think this is a confusing point because you are usually the main character in your dreams. But, there are times you will have a dream that you are watching a scenario play out, and the person you are watching actually represents yourself. For example, I had a correctional/warning dream once, and in it, I saw a family friend of mine pregnant. There was a lot more to the dream, but in the end, she gave me a huge egg with a stillborn baby in it. At first, I thought it was a demonic dream and that the enemy was trying to plant a seed of infertility over my life. I rebuked the dream upon waking, but since there was so much symbolism, I knew I had to fold, organize, and put it away. To my surprise, it was a God dream, and He was rebuking me for almost *aborting* a blessing He promised to send my way. My family friend was not a demon, but she represented myself.

Since we know that dreams are very self-centered and the majority of the time about the dreamer, it should come as no surprise that the scenarios that play out in dreams usually refer to the life of the dreamer. If that's the case, then how do we know when a particular character in a dream represents ourselves? I wish the answer was simple, but unfortunately, it's not. Since many characters can represent personal symbols, there's no formula I can give to determine if a character represents you in a dream because there are too many nuances. The only correlation I have witnessed through interpreting dreams is that the characters who accompany you in doing something in a dream may represent you and an area of your life. Many times the characters escorting you in a task, journey, or action, can represent yourself. Possibly the trait they hold represents that part of your life. For example, let's say you have a cousin named Faith accompanying you on a road trip in a dream. She could represent *your* faith journey.

A Character Representing God

Dreams are a common way God speaks to us, so it's no surprise that He would use symbols to portray Himself. Depending on the Person in the Godhead, a character can represent each one.

God the Father

Father

It should come as no surprise that God the Father would show up as our earthly father in dreams. Throughout scripture, God has always chosen a Father figure to represent Himself for us to relate to Him. Unfortunately, since many of us have broken relationships with our earthly father, we sometimes don't automatically correlate our earthly father to our Heavenly Father in our dreams.

Judge

God the Father is referenced as a Judge many times in scripture (Isa 33:22), especially throughout the Old Testament. Through the prophets, God promised to judge the disobedience of the Israelites as well as disobedience of neighboring nations. If in a dream you are on trial, many times the Judge can represent God the Father, your Lawyer may represent Jesus Christ (1 Tim 2:5), and the opponent may represent the enemy.

Male Role Model

Sometimes God the Father may show up as a male role model in your dreams. Since it is not uncommon for many people to suffer from father wounds (soul wounds inflicted knowingly or unknowingly by a father), God the Father may also be represented by an uncle, another male caretaker, or a male leader that you look up to.

King/Natural Ruler

God the Father is the ruler over all the land (2 Chron 20:6), and His Son is referred to as the King of kings and the Lord of lords (Rev 19:16). God the Father is the original lawgiver and government. If in a dream, you see a King or someone in government, sometimes it may be a representation of God the Father or Jesus Christ.

Jesus Christ

Servant

Many people overlook the fact that Jesus didn't come to earth to be served but *to serve* (Mat 20:28). It should come as no surprise that Jesus may choose to portray Himself as a janitor, worker, or contractor in our dreams.

Doctor

During His ministry, Jesus healed many people spiritually, mentally, and physically (Mat 8:16). Sometimes in a dream, He can be symbolized by a doctor, surgeon, physician, therapist, etc.

Teacher

Jesus's disciples referred to Him as *Rabbi* or *Rabboni* (John 3:2), which is Aramaic for *teacher*. Depending on what class you're in, God may be trying to teach you something, and that teacher represents Jesus.

Rescuer/Savior/Deliverer

As believers in Jesus Christ, our salvation comes from Him and His sacrifice for us (Acts 4:12). In dreams, Jesus may be represented as a warrior who saves you in battle, a firefighter, or just a character who saves you in a particular situation.

Holy Spirit

Mother

Hear me very clearly—the Holy Spirit is not a woman. The Holy Spirit is the Third Person of the Godhead and expresses Himself as a He. The reason He is often represented as a mother in dreams is that the attributes of the Spirit correlate with that of a mother. Sometimes, both of your parents can represent God the Father, and the Holy Spirit in dreams. As with all dreams, never cling to symbols. God represents Himself in many ways, so we may be able to relate to Him, but it does not mean He is that thing.

Moreover, just as we alluded to in a previous point, when a person has mother wounds (soul wounds inflicted by a mother knowingly or unknowingly), it is very difficult for that person to correlate his or her mother as the Holy Spirit in a dream.

Another Believer

The Holy Spirit dwells in each of us as born-again believers (John 3:5). Seeing another believer in a dream comforting, guiding, or instructing you could be a representation of the Holy Spirit through that person.

Coach/Mentor

One of the jobs of the Holy Spirit is to transform us into an image of Christ (2 Cor 3:18). The Holy Spirit does that by correcting and training us in righteousness. In a dream, if you see yourself working out and a personal trainer is coaching you, that could be a representation of the Spirit. Also, if there is a believer that you look up to and physically or virtually mentors you through avenues like social media and YouTube, they can also represent the Holy Spirit in dreams.

Characters Representing Angels

Angel visitations are spoken about throughout scriptures, and the Bible tells us that angels are ministering spirits sent to serve us (Heb 1:14). In dreams, angels can appear as actual spirits or as help through someone you don't know.

Some attributes of spirits who are angels in dreams:

- Wearing white or wearing light
- A warm glow or aura surrounding them

- Gives you messages
- Friendliness
- Helpful
- Points you back to God

Characters Representing Demons

As mentioned earlier in part one, demons can either show up in dreams overtly or covertly. Characters who are overt demons are demonic spirits themselves or someone who is doing something openly wicked to you (stabbing you, stealing from you, attacking you, or raping you). As stated previously, covert demonic characters are more tricky to spot and cannot be placed in one neat category. Covert demons can often seem familiar, unalarming, unharmful, and even friendly! The best way to discern if a character is covertly demonic is to *discern* the source of the dream first as we spoke about in part one. Please don't be paranoid and try to figure if every character in your dream is demonic before even discerning the source. That, in a way, is like putting the carriage before the horse. The source of the dream matters more than the characters themselves.

So, you may be thinking, *Okay that's all great but how can I tell if a character is a demon? I'm still a bit worried that I may get duped!* I hear ya. I think it'll be helpful to know what *type* of spirits are covertly demonic characters and understanding their strategies. This information may help you to understand how the enemy moves in dreams.

Monitoring Spirits

To begin, the kingdom of darkness is very calculated and orderly. In order to deceive you into believing a dream is not from the kingdom of darkness, demons will often mimic and copy the kingdom of light. Spiritually, there are specific demons assigned to every individual. Since you were born, particular demons have observed and followed you. Some have legal rights through generational curses and mindsets, while others are picked up through sin. Many people think once they become a believer that they no longer have to deal with demons. That couldn't be further from the truth. We are in a spiritual war (Eph 6:12), and we can either fight back and be victors or stay complacent and be victims.

When it comes to monitoring spirits, they are exactly what they sound like—*spirits that monitor you*. These spirits know who you are, who your family is, who your friends are, what you like, what you don't like, and everything in between. They can observe the things you struggle with and what you're accomplishing, and then they use this information to send strategic attacks to your life. They can even hear your prayers and wage war or delay what God has answered/released (Dan 10).

When it comes to monitoring spirits in your dreams, they can come in the form of people or animals following you or spying on you.

Familiar Spirits

So, without getting too technical, familiar spirits are a type of monitoring spirit. We often overlook them because familiar spirits are *spirits that are familiar to you*. In the natural and supernatural, they can come in the form of music, friends, acquaintances, loved ones, what you watch, and places you go. The primary function of a familiar spirit is *to deceive you*. They want to make you so comfortable and familiar with them that you forget or are deceived that what you're interacting with is, in fact, a demon.

Familiar spirits are also referred to as masquerading spirits, and the bible says that Satan himself masquerades as an angel of light (2 Cor 11:14). As it relates to dreams, familiar spirits usually *masquerade* as someone you know or something you are familiar with to deceive or distract you from their plot.

Some tips on discerning familiar/masquerading/covertly demonic spirits in dreams:

- Is this person shorter/taller/skinnier/fatter than they are in real life?
- Is this person acting entirely out of character?
- Is there something off about this person that you can't quite put your finger on?
- Does this person look like a caricature of himself or herself?
- Does this person shapeshift?
- Is this person wearing all black?

- Can you see their face, or are they trying to hide their face from you?
- Are they giving you something questionable in a dream (a gift but no occasion or no merit; a gift in bad condition; crumpled, dirty money; tainted food, etc.)?

These tips, in addition to the context you receive from the interpretation, will help you to discover if a character in a dream is a demon or not. I just want to remind you that these are just general tips to discern demons in dreams, but don't cling to them! Remember—context is key! I don't want you to use this list as an absolute guideline for every dream you have. Just promise me that you will lean on the Holy Spirit to help you discern characters. 'Kay? Good.

Characters Representing Symbols

If I can be honest for a moment, I'd say that the vast majority of the time characters in dreams don't actually represent a particular person but are instead symbols. Aside from characters in dreams representing heavenly beings or demons, they can also represent ideas, traits, events, phases, or other abstract concepts. The kinds of symbols a character can represent are varied and diverse, but from my experience, they usually have specific characteristics.

You may be wondering how in the world do you decipher if someone you see in a dream represents the literal person and not a symbol. To be honest, there's no cut and dry way to know for sure, but there are a few questions one must ask.

Do you have access to this person in real life?

This is a biggie. And when I say access, I'm not talking about you having their social media handle or being friends on Facebook. I'm talking about having regular access to this person and having some type of current relationship with them. For example, let's say that you see a close friend in a dream struggling with something that you didn't know about in real life. That person could be a literal character because you know that person in real life and you have a relationship.

Let's take another example. Let's say you have a dream, and in it, you see your best friend from kindergarten. In reality, you have not talked to this person in years. You may have them on social media, but you have not had a one-on-one conversation in an incredibly long time. Although it may be tempting to assume that the person in your dream represents a literal character, it mostly doesn't and is symbolic of something else.

Are you interacting with this person in the dream?

In a dream, can you see this person, but they can't see you? If you are watching a person from afar and they are unaware of your presence, then it may be an insight dream from the Lord. Perhaps God is revealing to you something about this person's life that He wants you to press in and intercede on that person's behalf.

Are you an intercessor?

Tying in with the last point, if the person in the dream actually represented that person in real life, there is a reason why God is showing it to you. Hear me very clearly—GOD IS NOT A GOSSIP! We have to be careful to not jump to the assumption that every person we see in a dream that we know in real life is a literal representation. The Lord is not in the business of spilling the tea to you if there was no reason behind it. If He gave you a literal dream involving someone else, then He's expecting you to take an action. Depending on the context of the dream, He may be showing you someone's character to warn you to guard your heart around them. Or He's showing you something that they are battling with because He wants you to fight for them through prayer. Whatever the action is, just remember the character of God and be led by His Spirit.

Family Members as Symbols

We've already mentioned how parents can sometimes be symbols for God, but what about when they represent something else? What about other family members? Oftentimes, family members in your dreams can be a literal representation of that person, but not always.

Before we go any further, I want to reemphasize the point of personal symbols. We'll discuss what family members can mean generally, but keep in mind that they can represent traits you associate with them. For example, if you have a cousin who is the black sheep in your family, they could represent something similar in your dream. If you have an aunt that always cheered you on, that aunt could symbolize support and encouragement in a dream.

Without further ado, here are some family symbols and their possible meanings:

- **Mother**: a nation (Hosea 4:5)
- **Brother/sister**: another brother or sister in Christ, a ministry
- **Son/daughter**: a blessing, idea, or opportunity that was birthed from you, people in a nation (Hosea 4:5)
- **Grandparents**: something old, generational, could also represent God as well
- **Extended family**: The Church or a ministry
- **Younger relatives**: can also represent something similar to children so, a blessing, idea, or opportunity that you are currently stewarding over

Friends as Symbols

A friend is also a symbol that can be literal, or he/she can be a representation of something else (See Common Traits as Symbols).

- One friend can usually represent all of your friends or the ones closest to you
- Something near and dear to you
- Sometimes they can represent yourself

People You Casually Know as a Symbol

Some characters pop up in your dream that you were never close with in the first place, or you only see this person from time to time. In that case, they can just represent your past, their most prominent trait, or your perception of them (See Common Traits as Symbols).

Your Past as Symbols

It is so common to have someone from your past randomly show up in your dreams. In the case of someone you were close with at one point in time and are no longer as close, this could represent many things. Depending on who it is (ex-boyfriend/girlfriend, ex-spouse, ex-best friend) and how the relationship ended (cordially or toxic), could determine if this symbol represents a past failure resurfacing. It can also be a marker that the theme of this dream refers to your past (could be a past insight dream from God).

Celebrities as Symbols

Raise your hand if you've ever seen Beyoncé in your dream! If you've ever seen celebrities in your dreams from time to time, then you're not alone. Usually, stars in dreams are not literal but symbolic and are highly personal symbols. What comes to mind when one person thinks of a celebrity will vary from what another person thinks. For example, when I see Beyoncé in a dream, I automatically think of worldliness or the world. For someone else who is a huge fan of Beyoncé and is part of the Beyhive, they might think of a queen or role model. So, since celebrities in dreams are personal symbols, when you see one in a dream, assume they represent the trait you think of when they first come to mind.

People Groups as Symbols

This subject is highly sensitive to some folks and can ruffle some feathers. Again, the dreamer is the best person to interpret the dream because many symbols will be personal. People groups are one of them. When you see someone in a dream that is a different group, race, nationality, or ethnicity than you, they usually represent the common trait that is subjective to the dreamer. For example, I had a dream once, and in it was a black couple who had just birthed an East Asian baby. Babies represent blessings, gifts, ideas, and opportunities. When I think of East Asians, the first thing that comes to mind is smart and foreign. So, that Asian baby represented a smart idea that was foreign to me.

Another example we can look at is cheerleaders. What comes to mind when you think of them? Some may think encouragement, some may think of snobbishness, and another may think of high school or college. As we can see, there are no right or wrong answers with personal symbols, y'all.

Let's take the last example: African people. As someone who immigrated from the African country Nigeria, I think of culture, tradition, and family when I see other Africans in a dream. For another person, they may think of poverty and lack. I know this may make some uncomfortable because no one wants to be rude or prejudiced, but it is what it is! Personal symbols are subjective.

Common Traits as Symbols

When you get stuck on what a character could represent, just remember that many characters are symbolic of the most significant trait they possess. So whether you see a person you know or a person with a specific title/occupation, sometimes it's best to assume that they represent the first trait that comes to mind.

For example, let's say you see a cop in a dream. What is a common trait that you would associate with cops? Perhaps you would think of something to do with law and justice because of their position in law enforcement. Hence, the cop could represent something along those lines (if the symbol is not personal).

Another example we could take a look at is ballerinas. If you saw one in a dream (and you are not a ballerina nor have you ever done ballet), what would you think? Again, you would probably think of a common trait based on what a ballerina does which is dancing or graceful.

Proper Names as Symbols

This one may be tricky if you're not someone who's into riddles. As mentioned earlier, God speaks in parables and is very poetic. It may surprise you, but sometimes names hold the symbol themselves!

I had a dream, and in it, someone was telling me about a girl named Amanda. In real life, I don't know anyone with that name, so I assumed the name was symbolic. At first, I thought maybe it represents a man with the initials D.A. because Amanda=A-Man-DA. Still, I did not know anyone with those initials, so I kept digging. I researched the meaning of the name, and it was "loveable," which made sense in the context of my dream. If someone in a dream possesses the name of someone you do not know in real life, try to research the meaning of the name and see if it fits within the context of your dream.

Also, names may be homophones (when words have the same pronunciation but different meanings), which may give the meaning of a symbol in a dream. I had a dream with the rapper, Ludacris, in it and understood it as representing something that is *ludicrous*.

Moreover, sometimes things are really simple, and the person's name in the dream represents the exact symbol. Some examples include names such as Faith, Hope, Grace, Mercy, and Comfort.

The same goes for cultural names in a native language as well. For example, I have a friend named Owolabi. His name is of Yoruba origin which literally means "money is birthed." When I see him in my dreams, it usually has to do with money or financial decisions in my life. Another example I'll give is when I dream of a family friend of mine named Anu. Her name is Yoruba as well which means "mercy." When I see her or her mother in my dreams, it usually represents something about God's grace and mercy in my life.

Lastly, sometimes proper names represent the name of someone else! *Huh?* Yeah, bruh. *Dreams be wild.* This actually happened to me a couple of times, and I was so annoyed. Imagine being confused, and the answer is right in front of your face. **facepalm** So let's say you have a dream of a person named Michael. That Michael might represent a completely different Michael that you know in real life. See, I'm trying to tell you that there is no formula to dream interpretation. You just have to be opened to the world of symbolism and lean on the Holy Spirit for understanding.

Transforming Characters

Ever have a dream that you or another character simply *transformed* in a dream? Yeah, it's more common than you think! Depending on the context, it can mean one of a couple of things. As we previously discussed, it could represent a demonic spirit shapeshifting into something else, perhaps to gain the dreamer's trust. There was a dream that I interpreted (See Examples) where a girl transformed into a woman the dreamer was close within the course of the dream. We found out at the end that it was a masquerading, familiar spirit.

Another possibility is that the transformation is symbolic of a spiritual transformation, whether the transformation is for the dreamer or another character. For example, if you see someone you know in a dream who has negative qualities transform into a person with positive qualities, then it may be a good symbol and can indicate a positive change. If it is the other way around, then that can indicate a negative change.

A friend came to me with a dream and she saw a guy she knew. Let's call him Femi. In real life, Femi is a believer but is not fully surrendered to Christ. He is lukewarm in his walk, and she has been praying for him. In the dream, he became another man who we'll call Charles. In the natural, Charles was what others would call a womanizer in college. He was very promiscuous, lost, and broken during his time in undergrad. Recently, however, he gave his life to Christ a couple of years ago and is completely sold out for Him. He started a ministry that encouraged other men to follow Jesus, and he uses his own testimony to reach young men his age. So, in the context of this friend's dream, Femi becoming Charles would be a positive, encouraging symbol. The dreamer's prayers for Femi were not in vain, and one day he will be more mature in his walk with God. Praise Jesus!

Lastly, it's important to note that a transforming character most likely will not represent God because God's character never changes (Num 23:19, Heb 13:8, Jas 1:17). Remember, our interpretations must hold up to the standard of the Word of God.

Messengers

This last one is relatively easy, and I wouldn't have mentioned it, but people ask this question from time to time. The question is, *what does a person giving me a message represent in a dream?* Unless the person had any distinguishable features in the dream, then this person is just a messenger. Sometimes, however, messengers in a dream could represent angels (if the source of the dream is from God and it fits into the context of the dream). This is especially true when you do not know the person in real life. The message and what they're saying is more important than the messenger himself or herself.

Common Experiences

Running away/getting chased

This is probably the most common dream activity that a person gets at least once in their lifetime. Depending on the context, this symbol can mean one of a few things.

One interpretation of running away in a dream is fear. The bible says, "The wicked flee though no one pursues, but the righteous are as bold as a lion (Prov 28:1)." A timid spirit may be the cause of fleeing in a dream, especially if it is a recurring dream.

The second possibility of this symbol is that it could be a soul dream revealing that you are avoiding something in the natural. Whether it's a confrontation or facing bad habits, these issues can reflect through running away in dreams.

The third likelihood of running away in dreams could be running from sin, generational curses, or destructive patterns. To be honest, this one didn't hit me until recently. I had a couple of people approach me dreams of this theme and the interpretation was them escaping some type of demonic "entanglement" (too soon?).

The fourth interpretation could be that the enemy is targeting you. As friends of God, we are automatically enemies of the kingdom of darkness. Sometimes the enemy wants to incite terror into your life through these nightmare-ish dreams. If the source of the fleeing dream is demonic or has many demonic elements, then it should be rebuked upon waking. Ask God for protection against what is trying to intimidate you.

The last and fifth possible interpretation of being chased in dreams is that it symbolizes spiritual vulnerability or weakness. Scripture tells us, "Be alert and of sober mind. Your enemy, the devil, prowls around like a roaring lion looking for someone to devour (1 Pet 5:8)." When we are not vigilant and are neglecting our spiritual walk, we run the risk of being prey to the enemy's schemes. This caution is especially true in dreams when this symbol includes a setting of war. If you find yourself running away during a battle, you have nothing to fight with, or you have an insufficient weapon, then it's essential to re-evaluate your spiritual walk. The bible tells us that the sword of the Spirit is the Word of God (Eph 6:17), meaning God's Word is the only offensive tool as far as spiritual warfare. Demons do not leave because of your shout but because of your *authority* (Acts 19:11-20). You gain authority by walking in your identity as a child of God, being washed by the Word, reading and applying the Word of God, and through intimacy with the Holy Spirit.

I cannot emphasize enough the importance of studying the Bible to sharpen your spiritual weapon. Also, If you don't have a weapon or you have the wrong weapons, being defenseless is indicative of not having enough scripture. When you lack knowledge and revelation of these things, it may manifest in your dreams by running away or through the use of weak weapons.

Falling

Falling dreams are another common dream element. Whether it was as minor as a trip or a stumble, or as drastic as falling off a cliff—the way one falls in a dream can provide more context as to what this symbol means.

If the source of the fall was an obstacle or a "stumbling block," then this is a biblical symbol. The Bible tells us in 1 Corinthians 8:9 that our freedom should not be a stumbling block to the weak. In essence, a stumbling block can refer to any sin, behavior, or mindset that can cause one to stumble or, in other words, fall into sin. So if you see yourself in a dream fall because of something you stumbled over, it could be a warning or correctional dream from God about something either you're engaging in that will lead you to sin or something that has been set in your path that will lead you to sin.

Stumbling without falling, in general, can simply be making a mistake, but it didn't destroy you. As humans, we make mistakes all the time, and we sometimes beat ourselves up about it and think there is no way we can be redeemed. If you have a dream where you stumbled, but you continued to walk, then take heart! God's grace and mercy are sufficient, and He wants you to continue in perseverance.

Falling, on the other hand, can have a different meaning. Being pushed, falling from a tall height, or falling into a depth can usually signify a lack of control of support. Also, where someone is falling from can give more context. If someone is falling off a tall height, like a building, it can indicate this person was in a high position and is losing control. Maybe the person is at what they perceive to be a stable place in life, but things are about to shake for them. If someone is falling into a pit, it may symbolize that person is about to or is currently falling into a low point in their life. That person could probably be experiencing a bad breakup, divorce, death, or depression. In any event, whether it's you or someone you know falling, these types of dreams should be taken with sincerity and urgency through prayer.

Laughing

Laughing is one of the symbols I believe most people overlook because it's such a common phenomenon in the natural. Paying attention to the person who laughs and what they are laughing at can provide an understanding of the meaning behind this.

When you are the one who is laughing in a dream, it can usually mean one of two things. It can mean being filled with joy/the Spirit or taking things too lightly and not seriously. You could be laughing because the situation at hand is genuinely bringing you joy, and you react to it. But, within my own dreams and others, there have been some dreams where the laughing was out of place. That usually symbolizes not taking something seriously. There are times God will give us an assignment or an important message, and our actions show that we either don't understand the severity of it or we do but are continuing in disobedience. Either way, we should press into messages like this.

Now, if others are laughing at you in a dream, it could represent arrogance or ignorance. Whether the people laughing are your "enemies" or not, it usually is not a positive symbol, especially if you are not laughing with them. In reality, when others laugh at us, it can bring about feelings of shame, embarrassment, humiliation, disgrace, hurt, and so on. Others laughing at you in a dream can represent something similar.

Fighting

So, fighting in dreams! What on earth does that mean (no rhyme intended)? Well depending on the type of fight (a simple verbal fight or a full-on war), the characters that are fighting, the source of the dream, and the setting, they can all give clues as to what a fight could represent.

First, let's talk about fighting monsters and demons. If the source is demonic, then this could definitely point to demonic attacks in real life. If this is the case, the next question you have to ask yourself is *what weapons was I carrying?* And *was I winning?* Let's be real. If you were getting your butt kicked in a dream, then it more than likely is not a good sign. As mentioned previously, having an insufficient weapon or being overcome in a dream could point to the need to build up one's spirit man.

Next thing—have you ever been so mad at someone that you wanted to fight them? Yeah, me too. If you're fighting a person you know in real life, then sometimes it could just be a soul dream, and you have some unresolved internal issues with this person that are manifesting in your dreams. Remember earlier how I said God can still speak through soul dreams? Well, in dreams like this, He's calling us to forgive. Fighting one another is not a godly attribute, and the Lord wants us to cast our cares on Him and to forgive one another as He has forgiven us. The Bible also tells us that vengeance is the Lord's, so don't carry out revenge on this person.

Lastly, fighting can also represent fighting in a spiritual battle and be a warfare dream from the Lord. If you're competing in a war or some combat sport, then it can point to spiritual warfare or some struggle that is taking place in real life.

Waiting in Line

I've experienced so many dreams of myself waiting in line. Usually, this points to either patience, perseverance, or delay.

Let's say you have a dream, and you're waiting in line. After a while, a new route opens up that promises you something quicker, but it's not as good as what you were currently waiting in line for. This may point to the temptation to settle or accept a counterfeit blessing in a particular area in life. Whether it's a relationship, degree, or career opportunity, this may be a call from God to be patient and persevere. Both of which are part of the fruit of the Spirit.

So we've covered waiting in line as a symbol of patience and perseverance, but what about it representing delay? Let's say you have a dream of waiting in line, and you or someone else is holding up the line, and the line gets longer. This type of scenario can represent delay, may point to something holding you up in real life, and may even signify others waiting on you. This could be something you're procrastinating on or being disobedient, or rebellious about. The exact meaning would depend on the context and other details that surround the dream.

Flying

I love flying dreams, and I'm speaking on flying dreams with no assistance from an aircraft. It's just you flying in the sky. This scenario is a generally good symbol and represents either going to a new height, soaring in the Spirit, or receiving a higher insight.

In practical terms, flying takes you from the ground to the sky, which is a higher level. This symbol could represent God bringing you to a new level in Him or a particular area in your life.

The next interpretation is soaring in the Spirit. Since the Holy Spirit is represented as a dove (Mat 3:16) and wind in scripture (*Holy Spirit* in Hebrew literally translates to *the Breath/Spirit of God*), flying could represent being taken to a new level spiritually through the Spirit. In the physical, you may begin to encounter supernatural experiences through the Spirit.

Another interpretation could be deliverance. If you have a dream that you are running away from something or someone dangerous and then you start flying, it could represent deliverance from your enemies. Praise God!

The last possibility of flying is receiving a higher insight. If we think about it, when you are at a higher height, we see things from a bird's eye view. We see things from a different point of view that we wouldn't usually see from the ground. This may be the case if the Lord is trying to show you a situation in reality from a well-rounded view that you otherwise wouldn't have seen before.

Being Late

I don't know about you, but dreams of being late make me nervous. I wake up in a panic, breathing heavily, thinking that I missed an important obligation or opportunity until I suddenly realize—it was a dream. These dreams are usually correctional or warning dreams. Sometimes I see dream interpreters try to soften the meaning of this symbol by saying these dreams are an encouragement to those expecting something to happen in a specific timeframe and a sign that the dreamer should be patient. I'm not doubting that this could be an interpretation within the context of a dream, but in my experience examining my dreams and those of others, it is typically a correctional or warning dream. That interpretation would make sense if the dreamer were early or on time to whatever event he or she is going to.

If we think about it, God is a God of seasons and divine timing. If God wanted to release a blessing to us at a particular time, I firmly believe He would tell us and would know if we would be able to be prepared for it. God is not trying to trick us, nor does He do things without telling His servants (Amos 3:7). If there was a place we had to be at a specific time, I highly doubt God would've told us last minute or knew we didn't have the means to get there. Being late for something in a dream usually means lacking in preparation for something God wants to release in your life. For example, God may want to propel you in ministry, marriage, parenthood, education, or career, but because you have not adequately prepared, you are late to where He wants you to be. I know many people will disagree with me and say that what's for them is for them, but that's not the complete truth. God may want marriage for you, but if you are not submitted to Him or properly preparing yourself for marriage, then it doesn't matter how much God wants marriage for you. You're not ready, and God will not release a blessing in the wrong season. We may get certain things within our own might, but God's blessings and timing are best.

Also, what you were late for can be an indication of the area of your life where God is trying to correct you. If you were late to class, then it could mean that you are late to learning something in an area of life. Maybe there's a certain lesson God needed you to learn, but you procrastinated on learning it, so now you're being delayed getting to the next place in life. Remember, God is a God of order. He will not take you to B if you have not done A. Being late for work can represent something similar. God could be telling you that you're late on something you have to work on. Maybe there's a project God wants you to work diligently on that you have neglected.

Being Lost

Being lost in dreams can sometimes correlate with being late or can have its own standalone meaning. Being lost usually represents confusion, discouragement, or setbacks, and can sometimes be soulish in essence. Let's say you have a dream that you were supposed to get to a certain place at a certain time, but you got lost along the way and then ended up being late. This scenario can indicate being derailed from a mission. In real life, it could look like God telling you to start a business, and you do, but then along the way you get discouraged and stop working on it. There could've been a specific blessing or opportunity God wanted to release at a particular time if you would've kept working diligently, but your vision got warped along the way.

Nakedness

Nakedness in dreams is one of the most common dream themes. Although it seems strange and uncomfortable, nudity in dreams is not always a negative thing. Similar to what nakedness represents in real life, nakedness in dreams means vulnerability or exposure. As human beings, we are very fragile and seek to protect ourselves most times. We would rather not open up to others (or even God, for that matter) even if it was to help us. On the other hand, sometimes we are vulnerable and naked in front of people in the wrong context. This can also be a possibility depending on the type of dream it is (correctional or warning dream from God, soul dream, etc.). Nakedness in dreams could also represent disgrace if the source is demonic.

Pregnancy, Birth & Babies

Another prevalent type of dream is dreaming about being pregnant or having babies/kids. Contrary to popular belief, pregnancy doesn't always mean literal pregnancy. It can at times, but the majority of the time, it's symbolic. Pregnancy in dreams represents preparing to "birth out something," conceiving an idea, or something expectant. It could be something new, an idea, an opportunity, or a blessing (Ps. 127:3).

Before I started my first business, I had multiple people (even a high school friend who is an unbeliever) who had dreams and visions of me heavily pregnant. Since I was single and celibate, I knew this wasn't a physical pregnancy, and my name is not Mary (get the joke?). It meant my business was on the brink of being birthed out.

If one was to dream of having a miscarriage, then that idea, opportunity, or blessing carries the risk of being aborted during the preparation season. This can be due to impatience, discouragement, or immaturity in the natural.

Babies and kids carry a similar connotation but represent a blessing, gift, or idea that has already been birthed out. Usually, babies and kids carry the weight of responsibility and stewardship. The age and the number of kids could represent the maturity of this blessing as well as how many blessings or gifts need to be stewarded over. A premature baby would express a blessing or idea that was birthed and released too early or before its time. A stillborn would represent an idea that was destroyed right before the brink of being released.

Romantic Encounters

Whew! The topic of romantic encounters is probably the most convoluted topic in dream interpretation! I believe this is so because this topic cannot be put neatly into one box. Sometimes romantic encounters in dreams can be literal, and sometimes they can be symbolic. Many times they can be soulish, and sometimes they can be from God or a demonic source. It's imperative to seek God to receive revelation from your dreams.

Before we go further, I want to explain the heart and mind of God briefly. When you receive a romantic dream, it's so important to know the character of God and that God will never contradict His Word. The interpretation and application of a dream should never be unbiblical. For example, if you have a dream that you are having a romantic encounter with a married person, the interpretation/application should never lean towards God suggesting to you to be with that person. That is adultery. Another example is fornication. Fornicating (having sex outside the confines of marriage) in a dream does not mean God is telling you to be with that person or pursue them in that way. That is sexual immorality.

Lastly, the symbolism behind the type of romantic encounter can be different depending on your romantic status (single, dating, in a relationship, married, widowed, etc.).

Attraction

So, you have a dream, and in it, you have some type of attraction to someone. Either one is attracted to the other, or there's just general chemistry going on between you two. If you know the person in real life, it could be a soul dream or an insight dream. However, we always want to err on the symbolic side first, especially if the person is someone you don't know in real life.

At the time of writing this, I've been having a slew of these types of dreams. I received the revelation that these dreams were representing a pending opportunity for me. That might sound like a weird conclusion to draw but think about it. When we are looking for a new home, job, or even partner, there are things that would *attract* us and things that would *repel* us. If in a dream, you have a mutual attraction to someone, it could represent finding what you're looking for in the natural. Maybe you're job hunting and then have a dream of mutual attraction with someone. It could point to finding a job that you enjoy and the job fulfilling your ideal requirements.

So, what happens when you're attracted to someone in a dream that you usually wouldn't be attracted to in real life? This type of scenario can indicate that the opportunity or blessing you're looking for is not going to be wrapped up the way you expect it. Let's say you're a young black woman who is generally attracted to tall black men, but in a dream, you are attracted to or dating a short white man.

This scenario could represent an opportunity coming in a way you least expect it.

Lastly, let's discuss when an attraction is not reciprocated. I had a dream that a guy liked me and asked me to help him interpret a dream. In the dream that I helped him to interpret, I was not interested or attracted to him (the irony!). Later on in the dream, I became attracted to another man, and the first man came and tried to get me back. I then had a vision (Inception, much?) that the first man became abusive later on. Needless to say, I continued in the dream with the second guy. To the average person, they would say that was a warning to watch out for men who will want to date me and become abusive later on, but that's not the case. God was speaking to me about a certain opportunity in the past that was presented to me, and I wasn't interested. Now there's a new opportunity that I am more fit for that will be presented to me, but there will be a temptation from an old opportunity to keep me. The vision of abuse was a warning not to get deceived, and I'll be miserable if I go back to or accept an old opportunity. I say all that to say that attraction in dreams does not automatically correlate to a soulish or demonic dream.

Intimacy

Now let's get into something more subtle, like intimacy. Some examples of intimacy in dreams can be lying in bed with someone, cuddling, holding hands, etc. From my experience, dreams like these are usually insight or warning dreams from God, especially if the person is someone you frequently see in real life.

For example, throughout my single season, I would, on occasion, have dreams that I would be in a bed with a guy I'm currently platonic with. These dreams would always continue with my male friend trying to cuddle or get more romantic with me, and I would feel uncomfortable and awkward. In the past, I would foolishly write those dreams off as "demonic," and I thought that the devil was trying to get in between my friendships. Lo and behold, it would always come to pass that the male friend was secretly attracted to me and would try to pursue something more. God was trying to give me insight and possibly warning me that I am getting too close with a guy, but I was blinded from seeing it. Now this is in no way the *only* interpretation of intimacy in dreams, but these types of insight dreams are something to look out for.

Another typical example of intimacy is if you are in bed (as in resting—not any funny business!) with your parents or family. Usually, this points to either intimacy with God (represented through your parents) or intimacy with a community, perhaps other believers.

The last example that I will give is one involving relationships. Let's say you are a young single woman that had a dream about being in a relationship with a nice gentleman. Now before I tell you a possible interpretation, you gotta promise me that you won't freak out. 'Kay? Alrighty. Sometimes a boyfriend in dreams could represent our Lord and Savior, Jesus Christ. I know, I know. That may sound perverted to some people, but is it really? In the Bible, Jesus is referred to as the bridegroom (Matthew 9:15), and the Church is referred to as His bride (Ephesians 5:25-27, Revelation 19:7, Revelation 21:2). As a young single woman, I have had dreams of having a boyfriend and sometimes that young man represented Jesus.

I remember having this dream of a guy, and we were mutually attracted to one another. He could've been my boyfriend in the dream, but it wasn't specified. I remember in the dream he was trying to get closer and more intimate with me (not sexually), but I pulled away because I was self-conscious of my body odor. *Basically, I thought I stank.* Now in real life, I was slacking a bit in my relationship with God. My schedule was crazy and when I did spend time with the Lord, it was a bit… shallow for a lack of better words. I recall doing praise and worship and would tap out before the Spirit of God could really come upon me and break me down in the presence of God. This dream represented my relationship with the Lord in the natural. Perhaps I was feeling guilty about some things and the Lord was lovingly trying to usher me back to Himself. Do you see? God does not have to be so confined to the limitations of our own expectations.

Kissing

Depending on who you are and your experience, kissing can relay different levels of intimacy. For some people and cultures, kissing and most forms of affection are reserved strictly for married folks. For others, kissing is a form of endearment or greeting and is commonplace. Biblically speaking, kissing can represent love, intimacy, affection (Song. 1:1-2), betrayal (Luke 22:48), reconciliation (Gen 33:4, 2 Sam 14:33), and brotherly love (Rom 16:16). Kissing in dreams can also represent agreement/covenant. On the other hand, kissing by ways of making out or passion could represent a soul dream or even a demonic dream depending on the context.

Weddings

Weddings in real life represent the coming together of two, a covenant, or a new beginning. Dreaming of a wedding usually carries a similar meaning. Although most people jump straight into a literal or a demonic interpretation, these types of dreams are often symbolic. Weddings in dreams can represent the start of a new season, job, career, ministry, friendship, opportunity, even a relationship. A bride can also symbolize the Church, and the groom can symbolize Jesus Christ (Rev. 21:9) (Matt. 9:15).

A friend of mine had a dream, and in it, she was supposed to get married to the famous comedian, Kevin Hart. She was waiting for him at the altar and she soon found out they couldn't get married. Other attendees of the wedding were consoling her, but she was not surprised or in despair. She was explaining to the other patrons that she couldn't marry him anyway because he was already married. Now in real life, she was in a brand-new season where she had just received a new job and was looking for a place to live with another friend. It came to pass that she moved in with this friend, and this person was struggling to make ends meet. This friend had a lot of financial obligations, and all of which put my friend in an uncomfortable predicament. Had she taken heed to this dream, she would have realized that it was an unwise decision to come into a new lease with someone who was financially unavailable.

Marriage

Unlike weddings, marriages represent something that is an ongoing commitment rather than a new beginning. Depending on who you are married to in the dream (even your spouse can be symbolic!) could give more clues. This symbol can represent a job, friendship, long term financial obligation, etc.

Adultery

Yikes! Adultery is not an exciting dream to have. Adultery in dreams can be literal or symbolic. If you are presently married and you have recurring dreams with your spouse cheating, then it can point to actual adultery. If you are not married or the person committing the act of adultery in the dream is not married or is married to someone else, then this can be a different meaning. Just as marriage in dreams can represent a commitment, adultery in dreams can represent a *break* in commitment or unfaithfulness. These dreams can represent unfaithfulness in a situation where you or another person was supposed to commit. This indication could symbolize your relationship with God, marriage, friendship, job, ministry, giving, etc.

Sex

Now we're here at the exciting stuff! So, sex in dreams is more complicated than one might think. In general, though, sex in dreams is usually soulish or demonic. But there are those rare occasions that sex in dreams is from God. And I know someone is ready to close this book and call me a hypocrite because "that's not biblical." Please hear me out. Depending on the type of sex being had, if penetration is involved, and if you know the person well or not, it can give more insight.

There are times that sexual dreams are actually warning dreams from God. God has given dreams that warn people of many things, and rape/sexual misconduct is one of them. It sounds farfetched, but is it really? I have actually interpreted a couple of sexual dreams where God was trying to warn the person of another's motive. One woman I spoke to had a dream where she had sex with a man she knew in real life. The whole time she didn't want it and wasn't feeling it but went along with it anyways. After ruling out the possibility of a spirit spouse (a spirit that is married to you), I began to ask her more about the man she slept with in the dream. She joked that he low key stalks her and is kind of possessive, but she didn't take it seriously. It then clicked that the dream was a prophetic warning dream from God, and He was warning her of a possible rape. I encouraged her to cut ties with this person and ensure her safety.

Here's another example of a sexual dream from God. Someone came to me with a dream, and in it, this person encountered an old love interest. It's important to note that in real life, this young lady believes that the guy struggles with many demonic influences. Anyways, she encountered him in a dream, and the man put a gun to her head, which she then proceeded to curse him out. When that didn't work, she tried to seduce him, which led to him performing foreplay on her briefly before she told him to stop after she had gotten a quick enjoyment. He then reached into her vagina and broke something which let out the sound of a loud crack. Although this was only a snippet of her very elaborate dream, many people would've automatically ruled that out as a demonic dream. After I interpreted her entire dream (see Examples for the whole breakdown of this dream), we discovered that this was a correctional/warning dream from God and that the dream may not even relate to sex. Sometimes God will use disturbing imagery, metaphors, and themes to get your attention, so we should never immediately rule out "bad dreams" (even if sex is involved) as demonic dreams.

In the bible, God is said to warn and correct people in dreams as we see in the book of Job:

Job 33:14-18 NIV (New International Version)

*14 For God does speak—now one way, now another—
though no one perceives it.
15 In a dream, in a vision of the night,
when deep sleep falls on people
as they slumber in their beds,
16 he may speak in their ears
and terrify them with warnings,
17 to turn them from wrongdoing
and keep them from pride,
18 to preserve them from the pit,
their lives from perishing by the sword.[b]*

Also, biblical prophets used disturbing graphics to exemplify Israel's unfaithfulness to God as in the case of Ezekiel:

Ezekiel 16:25-26 NIV (New International Version)

25 At every street corner you built your lofty shrines and degraded your beauty, spreading your legs with increasing promiscuity to anyone who passed by. 26 You engaged in prostitution with the Egyptians, your neighbors with large genitals, and aroused my anger with your increasing promiscuity.

Ezekiel 23:17-21 NIV (New International Version)

17 Then the Babylonians came to her, to the bed of love, and in their lust they defiled her. After she had been defiled by them, she turned away from them in disgust. 18 When she carried on her prostitution openly and exposed her naked body, I turned away from her in disgust, just as I had turned away from her sister. 19 Yet she became more and more promiscuous as she recalled the days of her youth, when she was a prostitute in Egypt. 20 There she lusted after her lovers, whose genitals were like those of donkeys and whose emission was like that of horses. 21 So you longed for the lewdness of your youth, when in Egypt your bosom was caressed and your young breasts fondled.[c]

As we can see, graphic imagery is not always strictly demonic and can be in a God dream. I do want to stress and emphasize again that God does not condone sexual immorality. At all. From the verses we just read, it's very clear that God was correcting the Israelites and their promiscuity to other foreign gods. The tone that the prophet Ezekiel used was of righteous anger, not of encouragement or passivity. Sexual dreams from God are almost always correctional or warning dreams.

So that's a possibility of a God-given sex dream, but what about a soul sex dream? Sex can manifest differently in your dreams depending on where your love life is, and your thoughts, attitudes, and behaviors towards sex. When one engages in certain behaviors or frequently watches or listens to heavily sexualized content, it is not uncommon to see certain sexual themes in dreams. But even when we have a soul dream, it is still crucial for us to measure our dreams to the standard of the Bible and the character of God. If something does not measure up, then we must submit our fleshly ways and take captive every thought and make it obedient to Christ (2 Cor 10:5). It is not God's will for lust to drive us, and lust starts from the heart (Matt 5:28). Even if you are a virgin, it is imperative that you remain pure in heart and motives. We must submit our lustful desires to God through prayer and petition.

Moreover, there is such a thing as demonic sexual dreams, which is the assumption I believe most Christians gravitate to when they receive a sex dream. A demonic sexual dream usually follows the same criteria as other demonic dreams (See Dreams from Demons). In overt demonic sexual dreams, there is usually a feeling of actual penetration, fear, confusion, panic, terror, and other negative feelings. Many times, they can come as a dark spirit, and depending on if you have a gift of seeing or not, you may be able to see eyes, horns, and other features. Overtly sexual demonic dreams can also point to a spirit spouse. Spirit spouses can find their way into people's lives from birth or can enter through witchcraft or through dreams. Their job is to destroy lives and keep people from fruitful, godly marriages. My friends, recurring sexual dreams are demonic. They must be rebuked upon waking, combatted through spiritual warfare, and a fast should take place.

Lastly, demonic sexual dreams can be covert. If you see someone that you know in a dream having sex with you or trying to, it can be a familiar spirit trying to deceive you. Sex in real life does not just bind people physically but also spiritually as well. In the spiritual realm, sex between two people always follows this spiritual law: *the two will become one flesh* (Gen 2:24, Mat 19:5, Mark 10:8, Eph 5:31). This means that whenever two people engage in sex, they enter a covenant and are bound together as one body. This spiritual covenant is created *legally* when it happens within the confines of marriage. By contrast, it is created *illegally* when it happens outside of marriage. It's like signing your name on a legally binding document that you didn't read only to find out you gave away some of your rights.

Illegal sex (sex outside the covenant of marriage between a husband and a wife) can open a portal that demons can enter, and it can also possibly pass on generational curses. Dreams are no different. Demons know this law, so they use it to their advantage even while we sleep. Demons can pretend to be someone you know and are probably attracted to so that they can plant demonic seeds into your life. Remember, sex forms a covenant between two people. If you accept the sex in a dream and do not rebuke it upon waking, you agree with the action that took place.

If this has happened to you and you are worried after reading this, don't fear! The name of Jesus is the name above every other name, and at the mention of His name demons tremble! Although there is more help in the Appendix, if you have a demonic dream with sex involved, a simple action to take is to cancel it when you wake up. Simply say aloud, "I come out of agreement with that sexual dream in Jesus' name. I renounce anything the enemy has tried to plant in my life." Simple. Take heart, though. Jesus has overcome the world. You don't have to be scared of these things because the enemy is more scared of you than you are of him!

All in all, sex in dreams can come from all sources. We can receive sexual dreams from ourselves, demons, and even God. But with all that said, sex in dreams is rarely ever a good symbol no matter the source. The majority of the time, it is a negative symbol.

Death

Death is a sensitive topic for many people and can bring up feelings of pain, anger, and regret. If you are going through a loss in your life, I pray that you receive the comfort from God that you need. When it comes to the theme of death in dreams, it can be literal or symbolic, depending on the context.

Symbolic Death

Seeing someone die in a dream is already scary enough, but since we know dreams are usually symbolic, you can rest at ease that this may not be the case. Seeing someone die in a dream (even if it's you) often represents a situation or a season coming to an end, or the need for spiritual awakening (Eph. 2:5). Usually, if there is no blood, then it's probably a symbolic dream.

Literal Death

Although I believe that when most people dream of death, it's symbolic, there are times when God is showing or warning someone about imminent death. These are usually warning dreams or closure dreams.

Warning Death Dreams

If you see someone you know dying in a dream, or if you see them in a casket at a funeral, then this could be a warning death dream. Before you start to freak out, though, let's go through a checklist first to see if this is the case.

- Are you close to this person, and do you have regular access to this person? This is very important to gauge if the dream is symbolic or not. For example, if you see a celebrity or an old friend pass away in a dream, then it's most likely symbolic.
- Where is your spiritual life currently? This is not to make comparisons or null anyone's salvation but judge for yourself. Are you in the right standing with God and actively seeking Him? Are you studying your Word and have a fruitful relationship with Him? These questions are essential to answer because of the character of God. He doesn't just give revelations to anyone who cannot handle or steward over it. It would be rare for Him to give a warning death dream about someone else to a new believer/baby Christian because they will not know how to steward over it properly. For someone who is not spiritually mature, God may still be trying to deal with that individual before He starts exposing other people to that person.
- Lastly, are you an intercessor? Every Christian is called to intercede, stand in the gap, and pray for others, but is this your lifestyle? As mentioned in the last point, it is rare for God to give heavy

revelations to those who cannot steward over it properly. If this is a literal warning death dream, then there is a weight and responsibility attached to it. If you are someone God has called to intercede, especially for other saints, then don't take these types of dreams lightly and pray against them. If you are woken up in the middle of the night often (sometimes at the same time every night), then take it seriously and go to war. Pray, fast, and share with that person only if led by the Spirit.

Closure Death Dreams

Sometimes people have dreams where someone who is currently ill or hospitalized passes away. These can be closure dreams from God, and many times these are peaceful dreams even if the dreamer is unsettled. Some have recorded dreams where their loved one is taken away by angels, or they are able to reconcile with that person before they pass. As mentioned earlier, God cares about you and your wellbeing. Sometimes He will give us these dreams to console, prepare, and comfort us.

Dead People

So, we've covered people dying in dreams, but about dreams of people who are already dead? Unless this person is a dead celebrity (i.e., Michael Jackson, Marilyn Munroe, Elvis Presley), then they could represent a familiar/masquerading spirit. Demons will masquerade as our loved ones to gain our trust and plant demonic seeds in our lives. If you dream of dead relatives giving you something in a dream, it's probably a trick from the enemy and should be rebuked upon waking. In the Bible, necromancy (contacting the dead) is heavily condemned, so we can assume the dead contacting us in dreams would be a form of necromancy (Leviticus 19:31) as well.

On the other hand, if a loved one has passed recently and a dreamer sees that person in a dream, it could sometimes be a soul dream. Perhaps the dreamer is still trying to process his or her own grief regarding the passing of that loved one.

Lastly, depending on the relationship a dreamer has to a person who passed and the context of the dream, it could be positive. For example, I had a woman who was recently widowed come to me with multiple dreams of her late husband. As we sorted out her dreams, she was pleasantly surprised to find out that they were all mostly encouragement dreams from God. Her late husband symbolized encouragement and love in these dreams.

Although there a *ton* more symbols to explore, we will pause here and continue to Part 4. You can find a symbol dictionary in the Appendix which includes colors, numbers, finances, settings, nature, houses, places, transportation, sports, human anatomy, clothes, food & drink, animals, and communication. If you're wondering why we can't go through them all one by one, it's because I don't want to overwhelm you! I know most of us are novice or intermediate dreamers, so I don't want you to have "analysis paralysis." That's basically when you overanalyze something so much that it discourages you from even starting. I truly believe with all the tools you've just gleaned, that you definitely have what it takes to crack the code! And besides. We don't cling to symbol dictionaries around here anyway. So, I hope you've been enjoying the ride because now we're about to put everything into practice!

Part Four | Let's Get Crackin'!

Introduction

So here we are folks! We've finally made it to the last part! Yay! You did it! In Part 4, we're going to put everything we've learned to practice and decode some dreams ourselves. I know. It seems a bit daunting with all the information we've just learned, but I'll hold your hand and we'll walk through this together. Below are some varied dreams that I have received over the years and the interpretations I've given to the dreamer. Keep in mind that many meanings of these symbols can be found in the Appendix. Use these examples, not as a copy and paste format for your own dreams, but see them as the Fold, Organize, and Put Away Method in action. Remember that every dream will be different, so always have a fresh pair of eyes when you encounter a new dream. With all that being said, *let's get crackin'*!

Examples

The following are examples of dreams I have received and encountered over the years and the interpretation. Certain names, dates, and personal information have been changed to protect the identity of the dreamer and are noted with an asterisk. Where there is uncertainty and "Maybe Faith" has been activated, there is a question mark (?).

Example 1: Airport

I was at the airport, and I had my bag and ticket ready. I went to the ticket agent and gave her my ticket. She told me, sorry, but I couldn't board. I asked her why, and she said because it's not time and that I must wait until August. In the dream, it was January, and my ticket had the correct date. I asked her why I had to wait eight months, and she told me because he's going to do something at that time. Then I woke up.

Fold

- **airport**: a place that connects one to his or her destiny, calling, or desired place
- **Bag and ticket ready**: prepared for a journey
    - Remember, don't look too deep into a symbol and pick apart what a bag and ticket mean. In the context of the dream, the emphasis is not placed on the individual

items, but together they represent preparedness.
- **Couldn't board**: cannot go to the desired place
- **Waiting until August**: August is the eighth month of the year, so perhaps it represents new beginnings?
- **It's January**: January is the first month of the year so maybe it represents primary?
- **Correct date**: everything seems to line up
- **He's going to do something**: God is going to do something special in that season
  - The "he" was not specified, so let's assume it's God

Organize

- The dreamer is at a place in life where she is preparing to embark on a new endeavor.
- Unfortunately, it's not the time to embark yet, although everything seems to be in order.
- She is currently in the beginning stages of something, or maybe something is not mature yet.
- She must wait on God to open that new door so that He can do something special in her life.

Put Away

This is an insight/encouragement dream from God. The dreamer is ready and prepared to go to the next stage in her life, but God is telling her to hold off and wait on Him. If she can be patient, God will do exceedingly abundantly all he or she can ever ask for or think of (Eph 3:20).

Example 2: Invitation to Wild Party

It was nighttime, and I was walking with Sharon*. While walking, a guy invited us to a party and handed us an invitation with a date on it. Sharon was very hesitant to go, but I wanted to go. We went to the party which was at a house where a lot of drinking, smoking, and sex was happening. I knew we had to leave, and I practically had to drag Sharon* out. Once we got out, the house collapsed. Sharon was so shaken up and was terrified to the point she was physically shaking. I was trying to encourage her, but then I realized I needed to go back to get the invitation. I went back to the rubble and picked up the invitation. I don't remember what date was on it.

Background Info:

- Sharon* was an old friend of the dreamer. They used to smoke weed and party together, but Sharon* is not an active part of the dreamer's life anymore.

Fold

- **Sharon***: the past?
- **Nighttime**: lack of clarity
- **Walking together**: in agreement
- **Invitation to a party**: an invitation to something
- **Sharon hesitated**: there is some hesitation to go to this place
- **House with debauchery**: evil, wicked, or perverse things happening in this place

- **Knew to leave**: a wake-up call, push to get out of the situation
- **Dragging Sharon* out**: she didn't want to leave. Maybe she had gotten comfortable?
- **House collapsed**: something destroyed, the reign of wickedness is over (Prov.14:11)
- **Sharon terrified**: PTSD, she is shaken up by the whole situation
- **Trying to encourage Sharon**: encouragement amid trauma
- **Realizing the need to go back to get the invitation**: recognizing the need to get to the root/origin
- **Got the invitation with date**: received clarity on where everything started

Organize

- There was a lack of clarity about something that happened in the past.
- Sharon*: the dreamer
    - Possibly represents herself from the past because they are walking together.
    - Since this is someone that she doesn't currently have a lot of access to, we can assume this person doesn't represent the literal symbol of Sharon*.
- There was a season in the dreamer's life where she was invited somewhere (perhaps some life event), but she knew something was off. She had reservations about going but went anyway.

- ○ The reservation could be about living with someone, a relationship, friendship, job, etc. Only the dreamer would know for sure what area this could hint to.
- She got to this new place and discovered it wasn't what she thought it to be. There was a lot of wickedness that happened this season.
- She finally got the wake-up call to leave even though something was holding her back. Perhaps she had gotten comfortable living with the dysfunction or enjoyed whatever this place or thing was offering.
- If she would've stayed any longer, it would've completely destroyed her. She got out just in the nick of time.
- Even though she got out, she was traumatized by the whole thing. She's been trying to pick herself back up, but she must understand the root of why everything happened. She's in the process of discovering how she got in the situation in the first place.
- The date may simply represent the date or period in her life when everything happened.

Put Away

This is a past insight dream from God. The dreamer went through some traumatic things in the past that she has not healed from. She must get to the root of what happened to receive healing and move forward.

Example 3: Fruit Tree

It was daytime, and I was at an intersection. Across the street was a tree that someone told me Meek Mill planted. I went to the tree, which was shaped like a pole and had a white ceiling on top. The tree also had fruit that I wanted to eat from. Two black guys were with me, and we were all trying to figure out how to get the fruit. They got two black plastic crates to create steps. While climbing on the crates, one guy stepped on my back to get higher, but it didn't work. We then tried throwing rocks at the fruit to dislodge them, but that did not work either. I then found a blue rod, almost like the plastic ones on brooms. I used the rod to reach the fruit, and then I woke up.

Fold

- **daytime**: clarity
- **intersection**: at a crossroads in life
- **A tree Meek Mill planted**: something about Jesus because He's meek or the tree of life
- **Pole with a white ceiling**: a limitation placed on this thing
- **fruit**: fruits of the Spirit, the fruit of one's labor, the result of something, blessings
- **Two black guys**: possibly represents the dreamer or spirits
- **Trying to figure out how to get the fruit**: trying to find a way to get certain things/results/blessings

- **Black plastic crates**: an idea (possibly bad, disadvantageous, or worldly because it's black) to reach the fruit
- **Guy stepping on dreamer's back**: this is burdening the dreamer (carrying a load on your back)
- **It didn't work**: no luck in this endeavor
- **Throwing rocks**: futile efforts
- **Blue rod**: a revelation of God, discipline

Organize

- Something is being brought to clarity and understanding.
- The dreamer is at a crossroads in her life.
- Perhaps she wants to reap the harvest of all God has for her in her life.
- There's a limit set on what she's trying to achieve.
  - God may be setting the limit because the ceiling was white.
- The dreamer wants to enjoy a particular result or blessing but does not know how to achieve it.
- The two guys could represent two ways the dreamer tried to achieve this thing.
- One way she tried to achieve this thing ended up being a more significant burden on her back.
- She has tried other ways, but they have been unsuccessful and futile.
- The dreamer must reach to God, receive revelation, and accept discipline in order to get this "fruit."

Put Away

This is an insight dream from God. The dreamer may be at a crossroads in her life and really wants to enjoy specific blessings. God is showing her that these desires are pushing her out of His will and into things that are cumbersome and futile. She may now be at her wit's end and is finally reaching out to God, receiving revelation, and accepting His discipline.

Example 4: Babysitter & Toddler

I was in my bedroom at night. There was a fair-skinned black woman (she could pass for white) in my room holding a newborn baby (perhaps she was a babysitter). There was also a toddler about three, four years old in the room. The toddler went to the lady, and the lady yelled at him to get away from her. I went over to the lady and told her not to treat him like that. I gave the little boy a hug and a kiss to feel special and not neglected. The woman was on the floor and fell asleep while holding the baby. I began fixing up the crib, which was abnormally very small and looked like a bassinet. While I was fixing up the crib, the little boy took the baby and brought the baby to me. He said, "Daddy puts the pillows over there because the baby doesn't sleep with them." Apparently, the baby didn't sleep on the pillows that were currently in the crib but usually sleeps with the pillow on the side of the crib. I told the little boy, thank you, and asked what he wanted to eat for lunch. I suggested a hotdog and went to the kitchen to make it, but I couldn't because there were dishes in the sink. I was washing the dishes, and then I woke up.

Background info:

- The fair-skinned, black woman is a personal symbol to the dream, and she thought of racism which stands for division.

Fold

- **Bedroom**: a place of intimacy in dreamer's life
- **Nighttime**: lack of clarity
- **Fair-skinned black woman**: division
- **Newborn baby**: something new, immaturity, blessing, gift
- **Toddler**: something a little older, something more established (3-4 years could be literal years)
- **Yelling at toddler**: treating the older thing with contempt, neglecting something older for something new
- **Giving the toddler a hug and a kiss**: the older thing is precious to the dreamer
- **Fell asleep with the baby in arms**: this new thing is overwhelming
- **Fixing crib**: preparing for the new thing
- **Small crib**: not enough capacity to hold the new thing
- **Toddler bringing baby**: the older thing is going to help with the new thing
- **Daddy**: could represent Father God
- **Pillow**: comfort
- **The pillow should be on the side**: put your comfort aside
- **Asking little boy what he wants for lunch**: trying to figure out how to nurture and support this old thing
- **Hotdog**: something quick and easy?
- **Kitchen**: a place of preparation

- **Dishes in the sink**: do not have the tools to prepare
- **Washing dishes**: preparing tools to be used, refinement

Organize

- There's an intimate part of this dreamer's life that lacks clarity.
- The fair-skinned woman represents herself, and she is divided probably between an old and a new thing in her life.
- She's been neglecting an old thing and has become overwhelmed with focusing solely on this new thing.
- She needs the old thing to help steward over the new thing.
- The dreamer does not have the capacity to steward over this new thing well, and God is telling her to put her comfort to the side.
- She's now trying to figure out how to take care of this old thing and wants something quick and easy.
- Unfortunately, she doesn't have the tools and resources ready, but she is currently preparing and getting the support she needs.

Put Away

This is an insight dream from God. The dreamer has something old that she's been neglecting, and she has been having a difficult time dividing her attention between an old and a new thing. This old thing will help with the new thing, but she must be prepared to put her comfort aside. She also doesn't have the capacity to support this new thing, and perhaps she feels like she is being stretched in this area, or she needs to think bigger about it. As she is trying to figure out how to steward over this thing, she's getting refined.

Example 5: Sexual Encounter

I was in my dorm room, and there was a funeral for someone who had recently passed away at my university. I was getting ready, and then I heard a scream outside my room. I ran out into the darkness but realized that there was no real threat, so I went back to my room. At the door to my room, there was an armed guard who was Stephan*. He waved a gun to my forehead and prevented me from going into my room. I started to curse him out, but when that didn't work, I was scared and apologized for being disrespectful. I became seductive and seduced him into a cuddle position. He began to perform foreplay on me, and although I knew it was wrong, I wanted to at least get one moan and pleasure out of it before I told him to stop. While we were doing this, I saw the word "S.I.N." in big letters over his head, and I told him to stop. He said, "Wait. In my lodge, we're instructed to break this." He reached inside of my vagina and broke something. The sound reminded me of crabs cracking before you eat them.

I went to the next room, and he followed me but was now in the form of a woman (I was still scared of him/her). I went to lay in the bed where my mom and sister, Ciara* were sleeping. They were already comfy in the bed, and I didn't want to disturb them, so I adjusted the bed slightly so that they could move over. Once they shifted and I laid next to them, Ciara* began to prophesy in the Spirit with so much authority. She began to call out Stephan* by asking, "Do you want your walk to be tarnished if you keep sinning *against your body?" Immediately, my mom looked at me and said, "You see?" I felt doomed and began to bow to my mother for her forgiveness, and she forgave me. Ciara* had another message, but I didn't want her to say it because my mom was there. Stephen* had fallen asleep, but Ciara* went to check if he really was sleeping because it seemed like he was faking it. We were all up now, and you can see the hate in Stephan*'s eyes toward Ciara*. To make conversation, I asked, "is it rude to call Ghanaian food poisonous?"*

We were now outside, and you heard the sound of orishas coming against us. Ciara* was alone at first, but then I joined her, and we sang in our native language. We were saying that God is superior to the orishas. My mother joined, and we all held hands. There were red, floatation devices swirling all around us really fast. I felt myself sinking, but once I said, "Jesus," I rose. Then I woke up.

Background Info:

- Stephan* is an old love interest of the dreamer. When she thinks of him, she correlates him with a demon or being demonic.
- Her sister, Ciara*, is not strong in her faith as she is in the dream. She is younger and looks up to the dreamer in real life.
- Her mother is not deep in her walk, either. She has a form of godliness but lacks the power thereof.

Fold

- **Dorm**: a place of learning, her life in the present since she is currently enrolled in university, or a season of her life
- **Funeral**: something ending or dying
- **Getting ready**: preparation
- **A scream**: something startling that distracts the dreamer or caused her to be fearful, or something to get her attention
- **Realizing no threat**: her worries are calmed, or maybe she does not heed whatever is trying to get her attention
- **Armed guard**: something preventing her from going back to her place of intimacy or comfortability
- **Stephan***: a demon, perhaps? Maybe it represents the past
- **Waving a gun to forehead**: intimidation
- **Cursing back**: fighting carnally (where is her own weapon?)
- **Apologizing and seducing**: giving in to something wicked, compromising
  - Note that it was the *dreamer* that was seducing, not the man
- **Cuddling & foreplay**: intimacy

- Perhaps this person represents a familiar spirit because she is comfortable with this man
- **She knew it was wrong but wanted the pleasure**: compromise, willingly engaging in a sinful behavior
- **The word SIN.**: pretty self-explanatory
- **"We're instructed to break something"**: it may be a demon with an agenda
- **Something broke within her**: engaging in this behavior caused something to break
  - Most would automatically connect this with barrenness, but we don't know yet. This could represent a different area of her life breaking.
  - So far, we don't know if this is literally sexual sin or just a sin being represented through the symbol of sex. We will find out later.
  - Remember—*Don't organize and put away while you fold!* All we are trying to do at this part is interpreting the symbols. Don't rush ahead and assume that you know what the dream means yet (See Folding Mistakes).
- **Going to a different room but this person is following**: entering a new place of intimacy, perhaps, but still struggling with this thing
- **Stephan* seemed to change into a woman**: this may be a masquerading spirit
- **Her mom**: her literal mom, the Holy Spirit, or someone nurturing

- **Her sister**: her literal sister, a sister in Christ, another believer
- **They were comfy, and she didn't want to disturb them**: the place she's coming into seems stable already, and she does not want to be a burden
  - Perhaps the dreamer is hiding this issue from others
- **She adjusts the bed and slides in**: she finds her place in this new season/place of intimacy
- **Her sister's prophecy**: a warning about compromising in her walk
  - *"Flee from sexual immorality. All other sins a person commits are outside the body, but whoever sins sexually, sins against their own body." 1 Corinthians 6:18 NIV*
  - This may be about sexual immorality since the scripture that was used is relating to that
- **Feeling doomed**: she doesn't want something exposed to either her mother or the Holy Spirit
- **Asking for forgiveness**: repentance
- **Stephan* asleep but Ciara* checking**: this thing seems dormant in the dreamer's life, but is it dead?
- **Hate against Ciara***: this spirit hates the sister for exposing it
- **The conversation about Ghanaian food**: the dreamer is creating a distraction
  - This is a personal symbol, but we can still get the context. In the midst of all that's happening, why would the dreamer divert the conversation to a lighthearted joke? Why

is the dreamer not attacking this thing or on the same page as the sister?
- **Orishas**: idols, demons
    - Orishas are Yoruba deities/gods.
- **God is superior**: God is bigger than any demon/idol
- **Red flotation devices**: saving grace
    - **Red**: the blood of Jesus
    - **Flotation devices**: something that rescues people from drowning
- **Sinking**: being overcome
- **Saying, Jesus, and rising**: through Christ, we are overcomers

Organize

- There was a season of the dreamer's life that ended.
- In the midst of preparing for something, something may have tried to get her attention.
- Perhaps she didn't understand, and she tried to go back to what she was doing.
- There was a familiar spirit blocking her from accessing this place
    - When we organize, we want to be able to put a name to those ambiguous symbols. From what we have folded, we can now assume that Stephan* represented a familiar, masquerading demon.
- The dreamer has tried to fight this spirit carnally, but it didn't work and she gave in to the temptation.

- The dreamer knows engaging in a specific activity/behavior is wrong, but maybe she thinks if she only participates in it a little bit, then she can have her cake and eat it too.
    - Sometimes we can think we're in the right standing because we're not *"as bad"* as others. We believe the lie that a small sin is not as bad as a "big" sin.
- Once she engaged in this thing, she was shown very clearly it was sin. She didn't flee, and the damage was already done.
- Her small involvement with sin caused something to get damaged in her life, which is a high price to pay.
    - We are not entirely sure what was damaged in the dreamer's life. Only the dreamer can fully apply the interpretation to whatever area it is in her life.
- She walked into a new sphere with this spirit still attached to her.
    - It could represent a friend group, church, ministry, or any place where there is a gathering and intimacy of believers.
- Someone sniffs out the sin and calls out how the dreamer is compromising in her walk.
    - Since her sister is not a firm believer in real life, we can assume that she represents a *sister* in Christ.
- The Holy Spirit is confirming what she may have already been warning the dreamer about this issue.

- - Again, since her mother is not a strong believer in real life, she could represent the Holy Spirit.
- The dreamer may feel guilt and condemnation. She probably hasn't confessed this thing to God and is trying to hide it from Him.
- She can repent, and God's forgiveness is available to her.
- Although she has repented, she is not free from this spirit. This spirit is dormant in her life, but it's not dead.
- The spirit has it in for the believer who exposed it.
- Instead of fighting against the spirit, the dreamer is trying to distract others from it.
- There may be a counterattack on the horizon, but the dreamer is encouraged to hold on to the truth that God is bigger than it.
- Even when the dreamer feels overcome through all of this, she has saving grace through Jesus Christ.

Put Away

This is a warning dream from God! When I explained the interpretation to the dreamer, it resonated with her spirit. The interesting thing though, was that she did not know what area of her life the dream was referring to. At the time of her dream, she was not engaged in any deep or hidden sin. However, as months went on the dream began to unfold itself, and she was tested in a very big way. Looking back on the dream and interpretation, it was very clear that this was a warning dream from God.

As I mentioned, it would be intuitive to assume the source was demonic automatically, but this was not the case. This is the reason why it is so important to sit with your dreams, not rush ahead, and fully interpret a dream to get the full revelation. In this dream, God is showing the dreamer that a familiar spirit is following her, and although she knows it, the dreamer does not want it exposed. This was also a warning that if she doesn't let this go, He will send someone else to expose it. There are also some soulish parts to this dream that expose the dreamer's heart as well. In the end, God's mercy is sufficient, and there is no condemnation for those who are in Christ Jesus. The dreamer is also encouraged to hold on to Jesus in the midst of everything that she's going through.

Example 6: Playing a Ouija Board

I was participating in a game where I was a slave. I was hiding under a bed, and there was a young lady in charge of me. I went to the bathroom, and it was pitch black. I reached for my phone to use the flashlight, and I had no idea that it was on this whole time. I put the light to the mirror to see my reflection because I felt like I couldn't see well with my eyes. In the mirror, I saw myself, but it wasn't myself. I had a lazy eye drooping downward, and my reflection smiled creepily back at me. It reminded me of a horror film. I freaked out and ran out of the bathroom, speaking in tongues.

I was back in the room, but there were more people now, and it looked like a get-together. The young lady that was in charge of me began to feel compassion for me and told everyone to put a few hundred in cash down for me. She wanted to be the example, so she put some money down first. The thing is, she didn't specify that it had to be American currency (USD). A few people put a couple of dollars down, but it was mixed currency.

It became nighttime, and I went to the bathroom again. When I came out, the young lady transformed into a good friend of mine, Miranda*, and she gave me gifts in a clear compartmentalized tray. There were so many goodies in there that I loved, and only someone who was paying close attention and observing me would know. I was so appreciative of the gift and thanked her. She also got me an Ouija board and told me to spin the wheel six times, and if *it lands on "p," then I can get my freedom. I was so happy and hugged Miranda* and everyone else in the room. Right when I was about to spin the board, a little girl in the room went to tell on me to the father of the house (who happened to be in the other room). He came, and I ran under the bed, but it was broken and falling apart. It felt like an earthquake was happening.*

I was found and about to be caught, but Miranda pleaded for me to play at least. I begrudgingly agreed and spun five times. When I was spinning, nothing happened, but the dad of the house was controlling the board and stopped the spin wherever he felt like. Finally, on the sixth spin, I landed on "p," and I was so excited. I was celebrating my freedom, but the dad didn't care, and I knew I was going to jail. The father carried me away, but Miranda was trying to prevent it and save me. She pleaded with the dad initially, but then completely switched up! It turns out she was evil this whole time and wanted me to go to jail. I was thrown in jail but had a feeling it was my fault, and I shouldn't have been playing the game in the first place.

Background Info:

- Miranda* is a good friend of the dreamer. She is a believer and a very sweet girl.
- A Ouija board is an object used in occultism.
- The dreamer has never played with a Ouija board before nor has she ever been involved with the occult.

Fold

- **Game**: the game of life, perhaps
- **Being a slave**: spiritual bondage
- **Hiding under the bed**: hiding under comfort
- **The young lady in charge**: possibly a spirit or represents the dreamer
- **Bathroom**: a place of cleansing, repentance
- **Pitch black**: ignorance
- **No idea flashlight was on**: could be ignorance that Jesus is always with the dreamer or revelation was always available
    - Jesus is known as the light of the world
    - Light *illuminates* something making it *clear*
- **Putting a light to the mirror**: Exposing the heart
- **Couldn't see well with own eyes**: ignorance with own understanding or insight
- **Seeing a reflection but it's not dreamer**: skewed perception of one's self or was unaware that is what the heart looks like
- **Lazy eye and creepy smile**: distorted vision, a wicked heart
- **Freaking out**: unbelief
- **Running out speaking in tongues**: could be the mundane habit of religion
    - Instead of confronting the reflection or repenting, the dreamer ran out speaking in tongues.

- Reminds me of when we pray, God reveals something to us, and instead of confronting the issue, we continue to "pray."
- **Get together**: gathering
- **Compassion and getting money together**: this spirit or dreamer feels bad for the situation she's in and wants to fix it
- **Being the example and putting money first**: establishing trust
- **No specification of currency/mixed currency**: confusion in finances or blessing
- **Only a few dollars**: this blessing is insignificant
- **Nighttime**: lack of clarity
- **Bathroom**: a place of cleansing and repentance
- **The woman transformed**: could be a masquerading spirit
- **Gifts**: certain things that the dreamer desires
- **Ouija board**: witchcraft/occultism
- **Spin six times to get freedom**: doing something in human strength to be free in some way
  - The number six represents man
- **"p"**: could mean anything. Maybe Promise Land?
- **Happiness**: deception that if the dreamer played this game, then she will be free
- **Little girl tattling to the father**: someone involves maybe God the Father
- **He came, and the dreamer ran under the bed**: running from conviction back to comfort
- **Bed breaking and earthquake**: instability in comfort

- **Being found**: being confronted
- **Pleading to play the game**: temptation
- **Agreeing to play**: falling into temptation
- **The dad stopped the spinner at will**: God is sovereign
- **Celebrating**: perceived freedom
- **Jail**: bondage
- **Miranda switches from trying to save the dreamer to condemning dreamer**: demonic familiar spirit
- **Being thrown in jail**: sharp rebuke, correction with consequences

Organize

- In the dreamer's life, she was in a place of spiritual bondage that that was hidden in her comfort. There's also a monitoring/familiar spirit over her.
- She went to a place of cleansing (could be in her personal, alone time with God), and God was trying to expose her heart. She was ignorant of the light she was carrying, as well as what the Lord was trying to reveal to her.
- When God tried to reveal her heart to her, she didn't like what she saw and fell back into a habit of religion due to a distorted vision and lack of understanding.
- The familiar spirit gained the trust of the dreamer and influenced others to give useless blessings that the dreamer perceived as true blessings.

- The dreamer went back to a place of sanctification, and when she came out, this masquerading spirit had gained the dreamer's trust. This spirit offered the dreamer everything the dreamer desired if she played along in this demonic game.
    - This is a personal symbol for the dreamer. Witchcraft is connected to doing things in one's own might outside of God. It also represents getting things one desires in an illegitimate way.
- The spirit was telling the dreamer everything she wanted to hear and appeased her itching ears.
- When she tried to play this game, God intervened, but she ran back to her comfort zone. Her comfort zone was crumbling, and her sense of security was gone.
- The spirit continued to tempt her, and she gave in out of fear. Although she kept trying in her own might, God is sovereign and continued to control her circumstances.
- When she kept trying to push against the grain, she hit what she perceived as a breakthrough, but it really wasn't.
- Going her own way would bring God's judgment on her, and this spirit is not on her side. She should've never entertained it.

Put Away

This is a correctional dream from God. Remember when I told you a basic template for correctional dreams are dreams in which the dreamer is willfully participating in something sinful? Yep. In this dream, this woman was engaging in an occultist game that she knew was wrong.

In reality, the dreamer came to the understanding that she was being influenced by worldly success, and she was seeking a level of freedom outside of God's will. The dreamer was also a slave to comfort, and God was trying to reveal her heart to her. She was ignorant, had a skewed perception about something, and was being influenced by worldly success. She ran from the truth and continued to be deceived by this spirit. This spirit has been monitoring her and knew her needs. It established trust with the dreamer and influenced others to give useless blessings to the dreamer that she perceived as real blessings. This spirit is offering her all the things her heart desires as long as she does it in her own way and strength outside of God. God and His love intervened, but she ran back to comfort instead of running to Him. She was continually tempted, then gave in and continued to seek ways to get what she wanted outside the will of God. She needed to learn that God is still sovereign, and there is nothing we can do that will trump His sovereignty.

When she finally thought she hit a breakthrough and was going to be propelled into her promised land, she got a sharp rebuke from God (which is probably this dream). The influence of worldly success is getting exposed in the dreamer's life, but she will face the consequences of her disobedience. All in all, this whole dream reminds me and parallels the temptations of Jesus in Luke 4. Jesus was tempted for 40 days by the devil and received the worst of it towards the end. He was tempted to turn a stone to bread, worship Satan, and to perform signs and wonders. In a way, the dreamer was going through her own temptations and didn't realize it. Although she may have failed her test(s), God can still certainly redeem her.

Example 7: Covertly Demonic School Dream

I was in my seventh-grade geography class in a high school setting. She was going over a class activity in which she would call upon different students to determine which state was which on a map. It was my turn, and I was having difficulties. I picked what I thought was New York or Connecticut, but said it was Maine. Immediately when I said that, I knew it was wrong and second guessed myself. To my surprise, my teacher said that I was correct and that I won. She handed me a prize and was so eager for me to accept it. The prize was a kid's goody bag with candy and small toys. I accepted the prize but was utterly confused. I knew I got the answer wrong.

Explanation

So, I know you were probably expecting a whole breakdown of this dream, but this is a covertly demonic dream. Our *Fold, Organize, and Put Away* method doesn't work as smoothly with demonic dreams as with God dreams. Like I said, the main gist to catch in covertly demonic dreams is the *feel* of them. Did you notice that *within* the dream the dreamer was confused? Yep. As silly as dreams may be to some, you are usually an active participant in whatever kooky stuff is happening, but this wasn't the case. This young woman knew *in* the dream that something was off.

Let's backtrack a bit and gather some essential information and context about this dream. First of all, why was this lady in her seventh-grade class in her high school building? The dreamer was in college and it seemed a bit odd. Next, the dreamer got the question wrong and *knew* it was wrong, so why was the teacher almost forcing a prize on her? The teacher lied and said she got the answer right even though it was incorrect. This whole dream could have been the enemy trying to plant seeds of regression and backwardness in the dreamer's life, possibly in the area of education.

All in all, you will know in your spirit that something is not right when you come across a covertly demonic dream. This is the reason why it's so important to lean on the Holy Spirit to determine the interpretation of dreams.

Conclusion

"We both had dreams," they answered, "but there is no one to interpret them." Then Joseph said to them, "Do not interpretations belong to God? Tell me your dreams." (Genesis 40:8)

This verse was monumental in my journey to cracking the dream code. In this story, Joseph was thrown in jail and encountered a baker and cupbearer who both had dreams but could not interpret them. Since I got saved and started my walk with Christ, *I* was the baker and cupbearer. I always had dreams, but not one person could understand them. I had no foundation or exposure to dream interpretation, and dreams just seemed like a bunch of mumbo jumbo. I had a feeling that some were from God because they would sometimes manifest in a weird way in real life, but it still wasn't enough.

This verse encapsulates the confusion that many of us had, but it also points us to the solution. Dear friend, I encourage you to seek God in your journey of dream interpretation because He alone holds the answer. It wasn't until I invited God into this area that He responded with a resource. Although my initial exposure to dream interpretation had some missing links, it was what I needed to start on this path. You may have been in the same boat and cried out to God for some help. Although this book will be an invaluable tool for your success in cracking the code, this book purposefully does not contain all the answers.

The Lord wants to show you deeper things and does not want you to overly depend on or idolize one particular source. *He* is the source and the primary Person you should run to for understanding.

You may be sitting here after reading this entire book and either feel a bit overwhelmed by all the information or genuinely enthusiastic to dive into the realm of dream interpretation. I want to encourage you never to forget God while you go on to grow in your gift of dream interpretation. Now that you have a strong foundation, the tools, and the resources to soar in this area, use it as a way to bond with the Lord on a more intimate level. Remember that you won't get it all in one go, and that's okay. It took me years and a lot of practice to get to this point and be fully confident in dream interpretation. Some of you may be quick learners and immediately grab these concepts, and some of you may be like me and need time to grow and develop. It's okay. Just know that this is not a race, and everyone grows at different paces. For others of us, we may have to deal with our perfectionism and heal to accelerate in this area. Keep striving, and don't lose hope! Remember that God's grace and mercy is sufficient for you.

Prayer

Dear Lord,

Thank you for this resource I have just received to grow in knowledge and understanding of dream interpretation. I pray that you will sharpen this gift within me, and it will be used for your glory. I come against any retaliation of the enemy from knowing that I have the key to understand what You are saying to me in my dreams. No longer will I perish from a lack of understanding, and no longer will I be ignorant of the devil's schemes in my life. I declare freedom from perfectionism, and I freely accept your grace in Jesus's name. Give me the discipline to not give up while I'm growing in this area, and to be patient in my understanding. Thank You for Your Son, Jesus Christ, through whom all things are possible, and thank You for Your Spirit that empowers us. All these things we pray in Jesus's name. Amen.

Do You Know Jesus?

So maybe you picked up this book because you needed help interpreting your dreams. You knew it was a Christian book, but there was something that drew you to read all the way to this point. Maybe you've heard of Jesus Christ before, but you never made the decision to follow Him. Or perhaps, you were raised in a church, but you never decided to follow Jesus for yourself. In any regard, the pages of this book may have compelled or convicted you to surrender to Jesus, but you're unsure of what it means or what to do next.

Dear friend, if you are someone who has never heard of the Good News (aka the Gospel), here it is. While we were sinners and eternally separated from God, Jesus Christ came to die for our sins, and in three days, He resurrected. The Bible says in Romans 10:9 that if we confess with our mouths that Jesus is Lord and believe in our hearts that God raised Him from the dead, then we will be saved! Isn't that wonderful news? It is our faith in Jesus Christ that saves us, and it is a free gift!

If you would like to follow Jesus, then repeat this prayer out loud. Remember, it's not the prayer that saves you, but it's your faith in the Savior.

Dear Father,

I now believe that Jesus Christ is Your only begotten Son, that He came down to our earth in the flesh and died on the cross to take away all of my sins and the sins of this world. I believe that Jesus Christ then rose from the dead on the third day to give all of us eternal life.

Lord Jesus,

I now confess to You all of the wrong and sinful things that I have ever done in my life. I ask that You please forgive me and wash away all of my sins by the blood that You have personally shed for me on the cross. I am now ready to accept You as my personal Lord and Savior. I now ask that You come into my life and live with me for all of eternity.

I now believe that I am truly saved and born again.

Thank You Father.

Thank You Jesus.

Appendix

Dream Dictionary

Introduction

This dream dictionary has been composed of the different symbols and their meaning that I've encountered through the Bible, personal experiences, other dream ministries, and straight from the Holy Spirit. As with all symbols, take this dream dictionary with a grain of salt. Always view symbols with fresh eyes and through the context of a dream. Never cling to symbols and attempt to derive formulas from their meanings. See this dream dictionary as a general guide and resource to help you to understand your dreams better.

Setting

The setting to your dream is incredibly important and can give greater context to your dreams.

Lighting

Let's discuss lighting in a dream. Was the lighting bright, dark, or dimly lit?

- **Bright**: exposure or something being exposed, clarity
- **Dark/pitch black**: demonic influences
- **Dimly lit**: being given insight on a situation that is unclear

Time of Day

Time of day can give more insight and context of the dream.

- **morning**: beginning of something
- **noon**: completion of a season
- **afternoon**: things currently happening
- **sunrise/sunset**: beginning a transition or ending a transition to the next season of your life, transition into clarity or the unknown
- **daytime**: clarity, something being exposed or brought to light

- **nighttime**: mystery, hidden things, not yet exposed, lack of clarity

Seasons

Seasons symbolize different spiritual seasons in our lives. When we see seasons in dreams, we can correlate it with what it means in real life. Another possibility is the holidays or feelings associated with that season.

- **winter**: a season of being hidden, isolated, maybe lacking or hardships, joy (Christmas time)
- **spring**: reaping a harvest, the beginning of fruitfulness and favor (Zech. 10:1)
- **summer**: enjoying the fruits of your labor, leisure, preparation (Prov. 6:8)
- **fall/autumn**: trials ahead (before winter), Thanksgiving/gratitude

Houses/Rooms & Their Content

Out of all the places you could be in a dream, your own home is the most common. Homes in dreams usually symbolize the life of the dreamer (Matt.12:43-44). There are some nuances that include family or ministry, but generally, when you dream of being in your own home, the dream is usually centered around your life.

So I only have one tip when it comes to interpreting homes. Often when we dream of homes, they are usually not our own, or they are, but there are extra rooms and features that are not in our current homes. I would encourage you to still assume it is your home/life, especially if dream you believes so in the dream. Don't get too caught up in the whimsical world of dreams and become distracted from what the dream is trying to communicate.

Now before we go into the contents of the different rooms themselves, we should discuss the different variations of houses and how they affect the meaning of the symbol.

Temporary homes

If we think about it in the natural world, we don't normally stay in temporary places for a long time. Usually, a rental home, hotel, or resort in a dream represents a temporary season in your life.

Unstable Homes

Unstable or poorly built homes usually lack the proper foundation and have a level of uncertainty attached to them. Dreaming of living in a shelter or a makeshift hut for example could symbolize instability.

Extended homes

If we understand a house to represent an individual's home, then it would make sense that an apartment complex, townhouse, neighborhood, or a city would represent many lives, or our lives connected to those around us. Now if you currently live in an apartment complex, then this may not apply to you. But, if you see yourself in either an apartment complex and you currently live in a house or a different apartment complex altogether, then it could mean your life connected to those around you.

Rooms & Their Contents

Bedrooms

Bedrooms represent rest and intimacy. If we understand that a house symbolizes a life, then the bedroom would be the most intimate part of us that others wouldn't normally see.

- **Bed**: intimacy, rest, covenant
- **Pillows**: comfort
- **Dresser**: something hidden
- **Lamp/light**: exposure, clarity, illumination, the Word of God (Ps. 119:105)

Bathrooms

When we think of bathrooms, we usually use them to freshen up, cleanse, dispose of our bodily waste, and other grooming and hygiene activities. Their meanings in dreams are no different. Bathrooms can represent preparation, sanctification, purification, repentance, self-examination, inner healing, or disposal of sin. In essence, bathrooms can represent the place where we commune with God and our spiritual walk.

- **Shower**: cleansing, washed by the Word of God (Ephesians 5:25-27), purification (1 John 1:7)
- **Sink**: washing, minor cleansing
- **Brushing teeth**: has to do with "cleaning" speech (Colossians 4:6)
- **Mirror**: self-examination, heart posture, motives, how you or others see yourself (Prov. 27:19)
- **Toilets**: disposal of undesirable/unwanted sin, behaviors, mindsets, etc.
- **Feces** (See Human Anatomy: Bodily Fluids)

Kitchens

Kitchens are where we store, handle, and prepare food, therefore represent a place of preparation. Finding yourself in a kitchen within a dream could mean that you're in a season of preparing something.

- **Stove**: conceiving an idea (cooking something up), something needs to be tested/purified (Zechariah 13:9, Psalm 66:10)
- **Fridge**: something that has been stored for later, something that will be picked back up or resumed at a later time
- **Oven**: something needs time to develop
    - **Taking something out the oven**: something that you have been waiting for is finally here and ready!
- **Sink**: washing, cleansing, purifying
    - **Dirty dishes**: neglect in an area of life, avoidance
    - **Washing dishes**: refining an idea, facing problems, problem-solving
- **Microwave**: something quick and easy, maybe ill-prepared
- **Freezer**: something at a standstill/ "frozen"
- **Cup**: being filled with something
    - **Cup filled with water**: being filled by the Holy Spirit (Ephesians 5:18)
    - **Dirty cup**: self-righteousness (Mat 23:25)
- **Plate/Dish**: serving, a group of people
- **Bowl**: fullness, completion

- o **Sharing a bowl**: intimacy, betrayal (Matthew 26:23)
- **Spoon**: conceiving something (*stirring* something up)
- **Fork**: investigating something (piercing, poking, probing)
- **Butter knife**: lacking spiritually (Eph 6:17)
- **Sharp knife**: verbal attacks
- **Wine glass**: communion (John 6:53-58), Jesus Christ

Living Rooms

Living rooms are generally places to commune, lounge, and interact with others.

- **TV**: viewing something, being shown something, insight
  - o What you're watching on tv can determine what is being shown to you.
  - o Watching tv can also refer to laziness and idleness (couch potato), or worldliness.
- **couch**: a place of comfort and rest
- **dusting**: attending to something that was neglected

Dining Rooms

As with living rooms, dining rooms can also represent a place of communing. What makes a dining room different from a living room, though, is the sharing of food. In this case, it can imply sharing or distributing ideas.

- **Table**: something exposed or made plain (lay it all out on the *table*)

Attics/Basements

This symbol might be cultural or regional, depending on who you ask. Personally, I've never seen a basement in dreams because it's not a common thing in South Florida (dig more than a few feet, and you might hit the water!). In any case, basements and attics in dreams usually depend on what the dreamer would attribute them to. They can sometimes represent your mind or internal issues that were never dealt with if you tend to view them as storage spaces. Basements can represent the same thing if you see them as extra storage spaces, or it can mean something underground/hidden. Since most people do not normally spend a lot of time in these areas, they can also represent hidden sin in the dreamer's life that is not exposed to others.

Garages

Now a garage is something I can relate to because I grew up with it in my home. Again, garages usually symbolize what you attribute them to. For me, my family always used it as an extra storage space, and it was usually filled with knickknacks, junk, and other things we didn't create a place for. If you see garages in this way, then they might represent something similar to an attic: unresolved internal issues. If you primarily attribute garages as a place to park your car, then it can hold a different meaning. Although we'll talk more in-depth about cars in the following section, cars can represent your life and *where you're going in life*. So, if you find yourself in a car inside a garage and you cannot get out, it may represent a blockage on your destiny or something hindering you from moving forward.

Closets

Closets, like dressers, are spaces/furniture to organize and store clothes. They can represent something hidden, as well, or a *prayer closet* where you spend alone time with God (Matthew 6:6).

Moreover, closets can hold cultural meanings as well. In the United States, the term *coming out of the closet* represents someone who is showing the world that they are part of the LGBTQA+ community. In this subjective case, a closet could represent *identity* or relating to LGBTQA+ for some people.

House Parts

- **roof**: covering, mind
    - **No roof**: no covering
    - **Roof caving in**: mental breakdown, attack on the mind

- o **A decaying/sagging roof**: laziness (Eccl. 10:18)
  - o **A leaking roof**: idleness (Eccl. 10:18)
- **ceiling**: mind, limitation
  - o Depending on what's on the ceiling can give you a clue about what's happening with the mind
  - o **Moldy ceiling**: attack on the mind, destructive mindsets
- **foundation**: foundational issues, back to basics, relating to generational things
- **windows**: insight, revelation, prophecy, future
- **doors**: access, transitioning from one place to another
  - o **Locked door**: no access
  - o The type of door can determine what type of access is taking place
  - o **Beaded door**: easy access
  - o **Steel door**: difficult access
- **walls**: privacy, transparency
  - o **No walls**: transparency, vulnerability
- **hallways**: transition
- **gates**: access
- **fence:** protection, being hedged in
- **Front yard**: things of the future
- **Backyard**: things of the past

Places

Probably after characters, places are one of the most important details in a dream. Most places we find ourselves in a dream are symbolic and are places we can recognize.

Unknown Places

Like I mentioned, we are usually able to recognize where we are in dreams, even if we are unsure of the exact location or are completely familiar with it in reality. In any case, there are some dreams that even in it, you are completely confused about where you are. If that's the case, this unknown place may represent confusion, or it just may not be that important to the general meaning of the dream.

Places of the Past

It's very common to dream of your past home, workplace, city, etc. These places can carry multiple meanings and sometimes are influenced by our feelings towards that place (similar to Characters: People from Your Past). Areas of the past can represent familiar spirits (demonic dreams), unresolved internal conflicts (soul dreams), or simply just your past. When I see places of my past, especially if it's a God dream, it's usually merely symbolic of my past and events that happened in that place. Sometimes God gives me a past insight dream of something that occurred in my past and builds up to how it affects my present and future. It could be a simple symbol for you as well.

Specific Places

Ever dream of a specific country, state, city, street? Similar to characters, specific places hold their meaning in their names, most prominent trait, or feelings associated with it. For example, I had a dream and part of it was that I was in Japan, documenting bizarre food. The dream was about my business, so I interpreted it as being in a place I've never been before that was foreign to me. It also meant that I was observing strange methods/ideologies in the realm of business. So, when it comes to places that you are familiar with in real life, assume the symbolic meaning is the first trait that you think of. Moreover, if I was to dream I was in Russia, as an American, the first thing I think of is war. Another person may think of home, culture, or tradition.

School/University/College/Class

I believe almost every consistent dreamer has dreamt that they are in an educational setting. As you may have figured, these symbols represent a place of learning. Depending on what is being taught, the class, or other clues can give you context on what you're learning. But, sometimes, it can simply represent a season in your life that you are learning and preparing for your future. On the flip side, if it's a demonic dream, it can represent regression and backwardness if the class or school is one that you have already passed. Lastly, the type of class or grade level can be personal. If you are currently enrolled in college and you dream of being on your college campus, it may hold a different meaning for someone who already graduated from college or has never been to college.

- **Late for school/class**: delayed in learning something
- **Forgot you were in class or had an assignment due**: fear of forgetting something that must be learned, unaware that current situations are a test and may have to repeat the test again
- **Grades**: how well you are doing in different areas of your life that God is testing you in
- **Skipping school**: avoiding learning something, irresponsibility, negligence
- **Graduating**: reaching a milestone, completion of a season
- **Elementary school**: learning the basics
- **Higher education**: learning advanced things

Hospital

Hospitals represent a place of healing, sickness, brokenness, or infirmity. This could be a church, ministry, etc. If you are in a hospital to give birth, then it could represent a place of "birthing" something new (See Common Experiences: Pregnancy/Babies). Being in the ICU (Intensive Care Unit) or emergency room would indicate something of urgency or needing great help.

Grocery Shops

Supermarkets generally mean a place of provisions or options. Depending on what you're buying can give context to the dream (See Food).

Restaurant

Restaurants are like dining rooms in houses, but there are usually more characters and activities involved. Restaurants can represent a place of communing, sharing and distributing ideas, serving, feasting, celebrating, or enjoying the fruits of your labor.

- **Waiting in line**: waiting to be served, receive an award or idea, or reach a certain milestone
- **Chef**: can represent God; someone in charge of preparing an idea, opportunity, insight, wisdom, etc.
- **Server**: can represent Jesus, someone who will come alongside to help you

Mall/Plaza

Malls can represent choices, provisions, or the world. Plazas hold similar meanings.

Specialty Store

Specialty stores are symbolic of what the store is selling.

- **Disney store**: the past, youth, childishness
- **Costume store**: not being truthful to yourself (wearing a mask), lack of identity, living a lie, pretending
- **Shoe store**: different choices, callings, destinies to "walk in"

Parties

Generally, parties represent celebrations or milestones. On the other hand, worldly/wild parties, clubs, and bars can represent a place of sin or the world.

Workplace

A workplace can represent your literal place of employment or can symbolize you are working for the Kingdom in your callings and purpose. It could also represent a project or hobby you are working on.

Gym

Gyms are places of preparation, strengthening, and endurance.

- **Personal trainer**: Holy Spirit
- **Unable to work out or working out is difficult**: unfit spiritually

Movies

Going to the movies or watching a movie can symbolize being shown something. Perhaps the dreamer is receiving more insight into something the movie or dream is portraying.

Parks/Picnics

Usually, parks represent a place of leisure or comfortability.

Cemetery

Cemeteries are usually connected to death, which is a loaded topic itself (See Death). Generally, cemeteries represent something that has died or ended (like a season in your life), something is spiritually dead (a grave in a church), or demonic altars involving witchcraft.

Jail/Prison

Being in jail represents bondage, slavery, or oppression. Being thrown into prison, on the other hand, can symbolize a rebuke and is probably tied to a correctional dream from God (Mat. 18:34).

Nature

Weather

Usually, the weather is typically temperate or unnoticeable in most dreams, but if you notice anything besides temperate, then you should consider it as symbolic.

- **Rain**: depression, an outpouring of something (good or bad), the floodgates of heaven opened (Malachi 3:10), blessing, cleansing (clear rain)
- **Storm**: trails, tribulations
    - **Storm clouds**: troubles ahead, ominous
    - **Hurricane**: troubles, distress (Ps. 107:28-29)
- **Rainbow**: promise, covenant (Gen. 9:13)
- **Earthquake**: instability, judgement, disaster
- **Snow**: cleansing, purity, grace
    - **Dirty snow**: impurity
    - **Blizzard**: lack of clarity, situation obstructing your vision
- **Stars**: heavenly beings (Rev. 1:20, Rev. 12:4)
- **Waves**: a move of God, trials, troubles, deceit, false teachings (Eph. 4:14)
- **Wind**: Holy Spirit (Acts 2:2), change (the *winds* of change), adversity
- **Fog**: uncertainty, a hazy situation, confusion
- **Tornado**: danger, judgement, major change, presence of God (Nah. 1:3)
    - **White tornado**: positive change

- **Hot**: passion
- **Cold**: apathy

Elements

- **Water**: Holy Spirit (if water is clear), refreshing, spiritual life
  - **Dirty water**: demonic spirits
  - **Moving water**: a move of the Spirit
  - **Ocean**: many people (Ps. 65:5-7)
  - **Lake**: smaller group of people, a group of believers
  - **River**: a move of God (if clear), or a move of the enemy (if dirty), blessings of God (Deut. 8:7), Holy Spirit (Jn. 7:38-39)
  - **Swimming pool**: a group of believers
  - **Beach/shore**: a place where we meet God
- **Ice/frozen**: something on hold, inactivity
- **Fire**: refinement, purification, on fire for God, judgement, destruction
- **Rocks/stones**: Jesus Christ, the Church, refuge (Ps. 31:1-3) obstacles, roadblocks, accusations/insults others hurl at you (2 Samuel 16:13)
- **Mud**: hopelessness, despair (Ps. 40:2)
- **Sand**: something that cannot be measured or quantified (Ps. 139:18),
- **Straw**: something final (i.e., That's the last *straw*! Or The *straw* that broke the camel's back.), lacking substance (Jer. 23:28)

- **Wheat**: legitimate (Jer. 23:28), God's word (Matt. 13:24)
- **Iron**: strength, getting sharpened (Prov. 27:17), judgement (Rev. 19:15, Ps. 2:9)
- **Pearls**: wisdom (*pearls* of wisdom), being caught by surprise (clutching my invisible *pearls*), something sacred or valuable (Matt. 7:6, 13:45)

Foliage

- **Rose**: love, romance
- **Lilies**: young women (Song. 2:2), flourishing (Hos 14:5)
- **Thorns**: worries (Matt. 13:7), Christ, suffering (Matt. 27:29)
- **Tree**: a person (Dan. 4), nation, prosperous/flourishing person (Ps. 52:8), wisdom (Prov. 3:18)
  - **Uprooted tree**: spiritually dead, false spiritual leader (Jude 1:12)
- **Vine**: Jesus Christ (Jn. 15:1), influence (Jer. 48:32)
  - **Wild vines**: laziness (Prov. 24:30-31), chaos
- **Willow tree**: weeping, mourning, sorrow (Ps. 137:2)

Shapes

- **Circle**: eternity, completion, perfection, cycles
- **Triangle**: The Trinity

- **Square**: grounded, stability, the world (the four corners of the Earth)

Mountain

Mountains pertain to many things, and it is mostly a biblical symbol. Mountains can represent obstacles, faith (Mat 17:20), or something to overcome. Being on top of a mountain can mean being at a high position or meeting with God (Ex. 19:20).

Cliff

Cliffs can mean you are hanging on to something that could be disastrous, or a dangerous situation.

Desert

Deserts can represent a wilderness season in your life, a place of trials and testing, or a place that lacks provision.

Forest

In the Bible, the word "wilderness" often provokes imagery of deserts. In reality, the Greek and Hebrew word points to *solitude*, rather than just a desert. A forest can represent a wilderness or isolation season in your life, as well.

Jungle

A jungle can represent a wilderness as well, or it can point to something wild, untamed, and chaotic.

The Arctic

The Arctic is another wilderness/isolation symbol. The only difference is that this place involves ice, so this can represent being frozen or stuck in a wilderness season.

Colors

Have you ever noticed specific colors or patterns in a dream? Colors may seem forgettable but can play a big role in adding context to our dreams. When it comes to seeing colors in dreams, they can be biblical, cultural, and personal symbols. If you are neutral to a color, assume it's a biblical symbol.

Lightness & Darkness of a Color

Sometimes the intensity of a color can represent the intensity of a symbol. For example, red can represent war. While coaching a friend, she saw a deep red in her dream, and I asked her what she thought it meant. She responded and said it reminded her of old blood. We were able to conclude that the deep red in her dream represented an old, difficult war in her life. Another example is the color pink. Pink can mean love, but hot pink can express lust.

Cultural Colors

Some colors have particular implications in different cultures. Depending on the country, a certain color can take on a different meaning that may not be universally known or biblical. For example, light blue and pink are synonymous with baby colors in the United States. So for someone who grew up in that culture, those colors could represent something in its early stages, immaturity, or childishness.

- White
    - Positive: purity, righteousness (Rev. 3:5), angels (Mark 16:5), forgiveness (Ps. 51:7; Isa. 1:18), victory (Rev 6:2)
    - Negative: religious spirit
- Black
    - Mystery, unknown, not clear, something that hasn't been fully revealed
    - Negative: sin, famine, death, evil, wickedness, judgement (Mic 3:6), hell (Jude 13, 2 Pet. 2:17)
- Red
    - Positive: Blood of Jesus (John 6:55), wisdom, power
    - Negative: warfare (Rev. 6:4), destruction, anger/rage (Isa. 63:2-3), Satan (Rev 12:3), target
- Blue
    - Positive: revelation, communion, spiritual authority/priesthood (Ex 28: 5-6, 8, 15), heaven (Ex 24:10)
    - Negative: depression, sadness, feeling low or "blue"
- Green
    - Positive: growth (plants/vegetation) (Jer. 17:8), prosperity (crops/money), rest (Psa. 23:2-3)
    - Negative: greed, envy, jealousy

- Orange/Amber
  - Positive: perseverance, persistence, presence of God (Ez. 1:4, Ez. 1:27)
  - Negative: stubbornness, danger, caution
- Purple
  - Positive: royalty (Lam. 4:5)
  - Negative: false authority (Rev 17:4), oppression
- Brown
  - Positive: humility (Adam was taken from the dust of the ground), compassion
  - Negative: earthly wisdom, compromise
- Grey
  - Positive: maturity (like grey hair)
  - Negative: compromise, lukewarmness (black mixed with white), death (Rev 6:8), sadness, weakness (Hos 7:9)
- Silver
  - Positive: redemption, refinement (Prov 25:4), high value
  - Negative: legalism
- Gold/Yellow
  - Positive: high value, glory, light, purity, prosperity, wisdom, purification (1 Pet 1:7)
  - Negative: materialism, idolatry
- Transparent
  - Transparency, vulnerability, clarity, exposure
- Rainbow

- Positive: promise (Gen 9:13), favor (Gen 37:3)
- Negative: prideful (LGBTQ pride)
• Neon
  - Attracting attention

Numbers

As you've probably guessed it, numbers are highly symbolic in dreams. Unlike colors, numbers are usually biblical rather than personal in dreams. Most likely, it's because many people are neutral when it comes to numbers. In any regard, there are still some personal numbers symbols we will cover in this section.

Dates & Amounts of Time

There are times we will see or be given a certain date or amount of time in a dream. Unless you are having an open vision, assume these markers are symbolic if you are a novice. I made this mistake often at the beginning of my journey in dream interpretation. I would receive a message in a dream with a certain amount of time or a specific date and see it as literal. Not to mention, I was sorely disappointed when that amount of time would elapse or that date would come, and I didn't see what I thought was promised to me. I say all this to say, whenever you see an upcoming date or a certain amount of time in a dream, assume it's symbolic before exploring it as a literal option.

Some examples:

- **November 18**: 11/18= transition and preparation
- **In six months**: after you let go of your own human strength
- **Noon**: completion of a season

Personal Numbers as Symbols

If you ever see a sequence of numbers in a dream that is significant in your life, assume that symbol is referring to the person or event it represents.

- Your personal phone number, address, or birthday are symbolic of your own life.
- A string of numbers could be the date of something significant in your life and can represent that thing (marriage anniversary, death of a loved one, or a milestone in your life).
- A string of numbers could also represent a national event or holiday and the feelings that accompany it (9/11: war or state of emergency; 12/25: Christmas, Jesus Christ, joy).
- A string of numbers may be a cultural symbol and can carry the meaning of the symbol (911: emergency in the United States, something is an emergency and should be taken seriously; 13: misfortune in many countries).

Area Codes

A possible interpretation of a string of numbers in a dream is that it could represent an area code of a place. Area codes can represent someone who lives in that area, a ministry God is calling you to, or a place God wants you to pray over. The possibilities are endless.

Bible Verses

Since God gives dreams sometimes, it is not uncommon for Him to use numbers to symbolize different bible verses. Again, the purpose of God dreams is for you to seek Him out, get understanding, and grow in intimacy with Him. If you see a three or four-digit number that is unfamiliar to you in a dream, try researching "bible verse (insert digits here)" to see if a popular scripture comes up.

- **316**: John 3:16
- **2911**: Jeremiah 29:11
- **121**: Psalm 121

Repeating Numbers/Patterns

Repeating numbers and patterns are very common. This could mean either God is establishing a matter, God is showing us something, or there is a revelation within a revelation.

- **1, 2, 3…** (ascending): order, God ordering your steps, increase
- **10, 9, 8…** (descending): backwardness, returning to basics, decrease
- **2, 2, 2**: triple confirmation
- **5, 5, 5**: triple grace
- **11, 11**: transition within transition

Numbers with Zeros

Usually, when you see a number with zeros, especially if it's a monetary value, it can represent the first digits before the zeros. For example, if I receive $500 in a dream, I am receiving a lot of grace because 5 is the number of grace. So, numbers with many zeros can signify a large amount of the first digit, more significance, or more impact. There are some nuances, especially if the number is biblical, but keep this in mind as a possibility.

- **1**: God (Deut. 6:4), unity (1 Cor 12, Acts 4:32, Mt 23:8-10) or primacy (Deut. 6:4, Mk 12:29, Jn 17: 21-23)
- **2**: covenant, agreement, confirmation, unity (Lk.10:1-3), choices, division, separation
- **3**: completeness, an established pattern, the Trinity (Matt. 28:19)
- **4**: creativity or seasons, the Earth/world (Rev 7:1)
- **5**: grace, redemption, fivefold ministry (Eph 4:11-13)
- **6**: man and human efforts (Gen. 1:26)
- **7**: completeness, totality, perfection (Gen 2:1-2), rest
- **8**: new beginnings
    - God created the world in seven days, so the eight day is a new week or new beginning.
- **9**: fruitfulness, fullness
    - Nine gifts of the Holy Spirit (1 Cor 12:7-11)
    - Nine fruits of the Spirit (Galatians 5:22-23)
    - A woman carries a baby for nine months

- **10**: the law, responsibility, test, and completeness
    - The Ten Commandments
    - The tithe (10%)
    - Ten plagues
- **11**: transition to next season, disorder, confusion
    - 11 is right before twelve
- **12**: completion, government, authority
    - Twelve months in a year
    - Twelve tribes of Israel
    - Twelve disciples
- **13**: misfortune (cultural)
- **14**: deliverance
    - The Israelites were delivered from bondage from Egypt on the Hebrew date, Nisan 14
- **15**: rest
    - The fifteen day of the Hebrew month, Nisan, begins the Feast of Unleavened Bread. The first day is a day of rest.
- **16**: love
    - sixteen attributes of God's love (1 Cor 13:4-8)
- **17**: victory
    - Jesus Christ conquered the grave and was resurrected on the Hebrew month, Nisan, day 17.
- **18**: transition and preparation, bondage
    - Jesus Christ transitioned and prepared for His ministry from age 12 to 30 (18 years)
    - The Israelites were in bondage for 18 years by the Moabites (Jdg. 3:14).

- o   A woman with a spirit of infirmity was bent over for 18 years (Luke 13:11)
- **20**: redemption
  - o   Jacob labored for 20 years under Laban until he was freed from his control.
  - o   It took Solomon 20 years to build the Temple.
- **21**: rebellion, an answered prayer
  - o   After God delivered the Israelites from Egypt, there were 21 major rebellious events that took place in the wilderness.
  - o   On the 21st day of the Hebrew month, Nisan, God pronounced the last judgement on the Egyptians, and they drowned in the Red Sea.
  - o   Daniel fasted for 21 days before he received an answer from God (Dan 10:1-21)
- **22**: The Word of God
  - o   22 letters in the Hebrew alphabet
  - o   The Bible contains 66 books (3 x 22)
  - o   22 chapter 22 in the Bible
- **23**: God is with us, refreshment, blessings
  - o   When 2 or 3 are gathered, there I am in the midst (Mat 18:20)
  - o   Psalm 23 is a popular psalm
- **24**: priesthood, authority, completion
  - o   24 elders on 24 thrones (Rev 4:4)
  - o   24 classifications of priests (1 Chron 24)
  - o   24 hours in a day

- **25**: grace upon grace, waiting and receiving a blessing
  - 5 (grace) x 5 (grace) = 25
  - Abraham waited 25 total years for the birth of Isaac
- **30**: the beginning of a ministry, betrayal
  - Jesus Christ started his earthly ministry at age 30.
  - Old Testament priests started serving at age 30 (Num 4:3)
  - Judas betrayed Jesus for 30 pieces of silver (Matt 26:15)
- **40**: testing, trials, probation period, a long period of time
  - The Israelites wandered in the wilderness for 40 years
  - Moses was on Mount Sinai for 40 days twice
  - Jesus was tempted in the wilderness by Satan while He fasted 40 days
  - Jonah preached in Nineveh for 40 days
  - Elijah went with no food for 40 days
  - 40 days and nights is a Hebrew expression that means a long time
- **50**: jubilation, freedom, liberty
  - Pentecost is the Hebrew word for 50
  - 50 is the year of jubilee
  - People were freed from debt every 50 years (Lev. 25:10)
- **70**: increased perfection

- 70 is a multiple of 7 (perfection)
  - 70 elders chosen by Moses (Num 11:16)
  - 70 years of a full human's lifespan (Ps 90:10, Isa 23:15)
  - 70 parables Jesus preached
  - 70 years of captivity in Babylon (Jer. 29:10, Dan. 9:2)
- **666**: full lawlessness, end times, Satan (Rev. 13:18)
- **888**: resurrection
  - 888 is the Gematria number for Jesus and symbolizes resurrection

Finances

There are times within our dreams we handle finances. As it pertains to dream interpretation, always assume finances in dreams are first symbolic before they are literal.

So what does money mean in dreams? Money in dreams can either mean blessings, curses, favor, misfortune, poverty, something of high value, or literal money.

Receiving/Losing Money

If you receive money in a dream from someone you know of good spirit, wearing bright colors, or a friendly demeanor, then you might receive a blessing or an increase in your life is coming. If in a dream someone is taking money from you, then it could be a demonic attack or you're getting robbed of something in your life. The context of the dream should give more insight.

Spirit of Poverty

Now let's discuss losing or getting robbed of money in the context of demonic dreams, especially recurring ones. If the source of a dream is demonic, then this could point to a spirit of poverty attacking you. The spirit of poverty is a real demon that either attacks people's finances or is attached to a bloodline (generational curse). This spirit is quite complicated for most to grasp because it's not just the state of being poor; it involves mindsets and patterns about money. It's vital to have knowledge and understanding about this spirit because it will help us to discern when this spirit is manifesting in our dreams.

Some traits of a spirit of poverty:

- Living paycheck to paycheck
- Everyone in the family struggles financially
- Making what most would consider a large amount of money but still never having enough
- Inability to save
- Financial illiteracy
- Does not practice giving/generosity
- Stingy/greedy
- Hoards
- Fear of lack
- An impoverished mindset
- Squanders money
- Orphan mentality (struggles with identity through sonship)
- Spends extravagantly/lives way above his or her means

Now we have defined some traits of a poverty spirit, let's see some examples of it in our dreams:

- Someone is stealing money from you

- You cannot find your money
- Holes in your pockets or money leaking from your bag/purse
- Begging/being a beggar
- Going to the bank, but it's locked or closed
- Unable to purchase things
- Having mixed currencies
- Spending money extravagantly and wastefully
- Trying to sell things but cannot sell

Transportation

In dreams, there's usually a *mode* to get us to the next place. Juxtaposed to reality, transportation in dreams usually symbolizes our life, family, ministry, or the direction we're going in life.

Cars

Cars, in general, symbolize your life and what's going on within it. Rule of thumb is that whoever is in the driver's seat is the one in control of the car/life. But don't fret if you see your parents in the driver or passenger seat; they may represent God. If it is an invisible force, then it can be a spirit (good or bad depending on the context). If your immediate family is in the car with you, this could represent your family. Lastly, the color of the car can hold significant context to what is portrayed. For example, a red car can symbolize war, passion, the blood of Christ, etc. A black car can represent sin, the enemy, mystery, ignorance, uncertainty or the unknown.

- **SUV, Jeep, or sturdy car**: well-equipped and prepared for what's ahead, something that is strong and can inflict damage
- **Beat up car**: troubles and trials
- **Car breaking down on the road**: delay either caused by the enemy or self, trials, unable to get to where you need to go, setbacks

- **Running out of gas**: lack of preparation
- **Stopping at gas station**: receiving provision for the journey ahead, being replenished by the Spirit
- **Roadside assistance**: help or aid
- **Car being towed**: receiving help, about to suffer a major loss
- **Flat tire**: setbacks, delay
- **Speeding**: being reckless, not taking proper precaution
- **Cannot control wheel or brakes**: lack of control
- **No seatbelt**: no covering or protection
- **Going to a mechanic or car in the shop**: receiving help, transformation
- **Getting pulled over by cops**: a rebuke
- **Car crash**: disagreement, dispute, fight, clashing with others, battle/conflict ahead
- **Rideshare (Uber/Lyft)**: you'll have to pay a price for this (Not always bad. Sometimes you must put more effort into something or make a sacrifice to get to where you are going)

Bikes

Bikes are usually single riders, so a bike is referring to the individual. Riding a bike on a highway though may represent inadequate provision to get to where you need to be, or it will take significantly longer to get to where you need to go. Bikes can also represent an individual ministry or endurance.

Buses

If we understand cars and bikes to represent an individual's life, then a bus would involve many lives trying to get to a common place. This is the reason why buses in dreams symbolize ministry, clubs, organizations, etc.

Trucks

Trucks usually take the meaning of the type they are in a dream.

- **Moving truck**: transition
- **Towing truck**: help or a big loss
- **Delivery truck**: deliverance/deliverance ministry
- **Food truck**: provision

Planes

Unlike road transportation, planes usually represent a bigger and faster change. Planes can represent a big project about to launch, a move, a business, a marriage, a ministry, and any other significant change in one's life.

- **Airport**: point of connection, transition before things take off (or not), a place that connects one to a destiny, calling, or desired place

- **Taking off**: about to launch, the beginning of something major
- **Landing**: the completion of something major
- **Taxiing**: waiting, preparing
- **Cannot take off**: not prepared to engage in an endeavor
- **Plane crash**: this endeavor will not end well or accomplish what it set out to
- **Turbulence**: a bumpy ride, discomfort (not always bad)

Trains

Trains have very similar meanings to planes, cars, and buses. They represent a fast move to another place.

- **Missing tracks**: not well thought out, danger ahead

Submarines

When we think of submarines, we think of a vehicle underwater. Submarines in dreams usually refer to hidden missions that the normal person does not see. This can be through behind the scenes work, ministry, and projects.

Spaceships

If submarines are underwater and undercover, then spaceships are out of this world and mean higher heights. Spaceships and space can refer to the prophetic/supernatural or accomplishing something that has never been done before, or not many people have achieved it.

Paths

In dreams, we are often walking, and we encounter different paths that mean different things.

Stairs/Escalators/Elevators/Slides

Out of all the paths you can take, these few are the most common. These paths have to do with elevation and can take you to a higher or lower level. They usually symbolize promotion/demotion, success/trials, or elevation/hardships. Escalators and elevations often express a quicker change in promotion or season, while a slide can represent immaturity or childishness.

Roads

Roads, very simply, represent journeys.

- **Dirt road**: hardships, trials
- **Smooth road**: a smooth journey, comfort
- **Bumpy road**: discomfort, trials
- **Narrow road**: the path of righteousness (Mat 7:14)
- **Crooked road**: confusion, unrighteousness (Isa. 59:8)
- **Maze**: confusion, being lost

- **Pothole**: a rough patch in life (a *bump* in the road)

Bridges

Bridges are connection points, and they connect you to where you need to go.

- **Broken bridge**: unable to get to where you need to be
- **Damaged bridge**: trials ahead, setbacks
- **Driving off a bridge**: unable to get to where you need to be possibly because of lack of control

Ground

If you ever notice the ground beneath your feet in a dream, chances are it's significant. The type of ground you're standing on can give insight into what's going on spiritually.

- **Shaky ground**: lack of control
- **Quicksand**: despair, danger (Ps. 69:2)
- **Sandy ground**: lack of solid foundation, disobedience, foolishness (Matthew 7:24-27)
- **Thorny ground**: foundation not deeply rooted, fear, unfruitfulness, shallow spiritual life (Mat 13: 22)
- **Rocky ground**: firm foundation (Matthew 7:24-25), lacking depth in spiritual walk (Mat 13: 20-21)
- **Soft soil**: obedient heart (Mat 13:23)
- **Tar**: a trap (Gen. 14:10)

Directions

What direction you're going in a dream can have significant implications, and most directional symbols are biblical.

- **Maps/GPS**: where you're going in life, directions/instructions
- **Left**: turning left symbolizes going the way of the world or human strength and wisdom, path of foolishness (Eccl. 10:2)
- **Right**: turning right in a dream symbolizes going the way of righteousness (Eccl. 10:2), literally right/correct, divine strength, faith
- **back**: things of the past (i.e., a backyard)
- **front**: things currently happening or yet to happen (i.e., a front yard)
- **north**: something going well, heaven
- **south**: something not going well (going south), hell, sin
- **west**: something starting
- **east**: something ending, last

Sports

I won't lie to you; I'm not the most active person. If it weren't for praise dancing, I would be a couch potato! Needless to say, I find myself participating in sports or at least watching them from time to time in my dreams. Many times, sports can represent spiritual warfare and involve a strategy to gain victory, or sports can just describe the game of life.

- **Basketball**: back and forth spiritual warfare, taller opponents can mean a stronger spiritual attack
- **Football**: spiritual warfare with longer periods of wins and losses
- **Soccer**: spiritual warfare requiring more endurance
- **Boxing**: taking hits in battle
- **Sliding sports**: something easy (as in skating on by)
    - **Ice skating**: something easy that will be done later (ice can represents being frozen in time)
    - **Skating on thin ice**: a dangerous and potentially disastrous situation
    - **Skateboarding**: something easy that will take some effort
    - **skiing/sledding**: something easy and fast

Human Anatomy

Out of all the things you would think to be literal, I bet you expected human anatomy to be one of them. Although I won't discredit some anatomy dreams signally something biological going on with us, in most dreams, these things are symbolic.

Head

Your head represents your insight, vision, and perspectives. A head can also symbolize a husband or Jesus Christ (Eph 5:23).

Hair

Hair was always a tricky symbol for me to understand when I first started interpreting dreams. The only thing I knew to connect to hair was the scripture that says a woman's hair is her glory (1 Cor 11:15). But can I be honest with you for a moment? I had no idea what glory really meant (don't judge me). Over the years, I have found hair in dreams to represent not only glory but wisdom and anointing. As with other symbols, the color of the hair can give more revelation on the symbol. For example, unusually black hair can represent worldly wisdom, false glory, sin, wrong perspective, or demonic attack on the mind. White hair can represent wisdom or maturity. Lastly, it's important to note that if someone usually wears wigs in real life, then the wig represents his or her hair in a dream.

- **Wig**: putting on something, taking on a certain perspective or mindset, false glory
- **Cutting hair**: transformation (if good dream), an attack on marriage (if the dreamer is a woman) (1 Cor 11:2-16)

Eyes

Eyes symbolize our perspective and how we view the world, as well as our vision.

- **Blurry vision**: lack of clarity
- **Cannot keep eyes open or in a slumber**: lack of awareness, lack of clarity, not keen to spiritual things

Nose

The nose represents discernment or being *nosy*.

- **Runny nose**: not discerning, unaware of what is happening in surroundings

Ears

Ears reflect our ability to hear and receive information.

- **Ears filled with earwax**: inability to hear God clearly (Isa. 6:10) or not guarding things listened to

Mouth

Mouths are used to break down food, which in the dream realm represents information. Mouths, therefore, represent our ability to break down information. Mouths can also reflect our speech.

- **Tongue**: speech, the gift of tongues
  - **Silver tongue**: righteousness (Prov.10:20)
- **Teeth**: wisdom, insight, speech
  - **Sharp teeth**: destructive speech (Ps. 57:4)
  - **Crooked teeth**: skewed understanding
  - **Missing teeth**: lacking understanding
- **Teeth falling out**: lack of wisdom, insight, or understanding, humiliation
- **Cold sores/canker sores**: destructive speech
- **Belching/burping**: harmful speech (Ps. 59:7)

Neck

If we think of the function of the neck in real life, we can see the neck supports the head. Necks represent support or strength (Job 41:22), while the throat can represent our speech.

- **Unable to speak**: inability to speak the Word of God, lack of spiritual authority, spiritual attack on voice (ability to speak up)

Limbs

Limbs are our extension to the world around us and give us mobility.

- **No limbs**: lack of mobility, stagnation, inability to move forward
- **Arms**: extension
- **Hands**: serving, work
    - **Right hand**: God's strength (Ex 15:6), favor (Psa. 16:11), help (Psa. 20:6), Jesus Christ (Mk 14:62)
- **Thigh**: faith, covenant, promise (Gen 24:2, 9, 47:29)
- **Legs**: strength (Song of Songs 5:15, Psalm 147:10)
- **Fingers**: ability to "grab hold" of something or the fivefold ministry
    - **Thumb**: apostle, anchor
    - **Index**: prophet, correction, conviction
    - **Middle**: evangelist, extension
    - **Ring**: pastor, covenant, marriage
    - **Pinky**: teacher, details

Torso

Our torsos house many of our vital organs.

- **Heart**: motives, intentions, commitment
    - **Stone heart**: unregenerate, calloused (Ezek. 36:26)
- **Lungs**: ability to take in things of the Spirit

- **Ribs**: protection, marriage
- **Stomach**: the ability to process something or "stomach" information
- **Back**: the past, dismissing something (Ps. 127:3)

Reproductive Organs

- **Breasts**: nurturing something
- **Genitals**: relating to sex, the ability to multiply or barrenness

Bodily Fluids

Bodily fluids can represent a variety of things, depending on which fluid is being released and the context of the dream. They can represent deliverance, cleansing, or spiritual/physical sickness.

- **Feces**: disposal of unwanted or undesirable sin, behaviors, mindsets, inner healing
  - **Defecating in a toilet**: normal and orderly removal, inner healing taking place
  - **Defecating on the floor or not in a toilet**: improper removal, negative outburst, loss of control or temper
  - **Defecating while others watching or lack of privacy**: others watching the process and aware of the inner healing taking place
  - **Colored stool (other than brown)**: the type of removal (for example, green stool can

represent the removal/purging of greed, envy, jealousy, etc.)
    - **Playing in stool**: returning to old ways
    - **Diapers**: assistance needed with inner healing or the removal of unwanted behaviors or mindsets, immaturity
- **Urination**: removal of excess, disgrace
- **Saliva**: processing something, understanding (saliva breaks down food)
    - **Swallowing**: the acceptance of something
- **Vomit**: not able to keep something down; not able to "digest" something like a word, message, or correction; purging harmful information such bad or improper doctrine, ideologies, mindsets; deliverance
    - **Eating or playing in vomit**: returning to sin (Prov. 26:11)
- **Mucus**: from nose means lack of discernment, from throat means speech is affected
    - **Phlegm**: apathy, indifference, sluggishness, self-composure
- **Menstrual cycle**: cleansing, purification, disgrace, humiliation

Bodily Imperfections

- **Acne**: the true essence of you, character flaws
- **Boils**: a curse (Ex 9:9)
- **Body odor**: an unrighteous life (Eph. 5:2)
- **Sores/Wound**: affliction (Isa. 3:17), sin (Ps. 38:5)
- **Scar**: an old wound, past hurts and trauma

Clothes

If you ever remember particular clothes in a dream, it is probably important. The type of clothing and the color can carry the significance of that symbol.

Cultural Clothes

If you see someone or yourself wearing cultural clothes in a dream, it probably speaks to the culture of that clothing and what it represents to the dreamer (See People Groups as Symbols).

Formalwear

Depending on the type of formalwear one is wearing, it can determine the type of symbol being portrayed.

- **Wedding dress**: covenant (See Romantic Encounters)
- **Party wear**: celebration, milestone
    - **Clubwear**: sin, debauchery
- **Business wear**: calling to a higher position or certain job
- **Ministry clothes**: calling to ministry

Sleepwear

We are in our most vulnerable state when we are sleeping and are often unaware of what's happening around us. In a dream, if you find yourself wearing sleepwear, then it could speak to something you are not aware of in reality. This is especially true if you are in sleepwear outside of the house or during an unfit occasion.

Bathrobe

Normally one would put on a bathrobe after they leave the bathroom. Bathrobes represent cleansing, purification, and healing.

Workout Clothes

When we think of working out, we think of training, strengthening, and preparing. This is especially true in dreams and represents training and preparation.

Bathing Suit

Bodies of water in dreams typically have to do with things of the Spirit, so a bathing suit would represent something similar. Bathing suits would symbolize our ability to move in the Spirit.

Underwear

In the natural realm, underwear covers our most private and intimate parts. The dream realm is no different, although underwear can sometimes speak to sexual purity or impurity. Black underwear in dreams can sometimes refer to sexual immorality while a black bra can represent sexual impurity or issues with nurturing and stewarding over something (See Human Anatomy: Breasts). Black and white underwear can also speak to sexual ambivalence, double-mindedness, or compromise.

Hats

Hats can represent a covering or a role the person is playing.

- **Helmet**: protection, salvation (Eph. 6:17)
- **Crown**: royalty, authority, dominion

Shoes

Shoes are probably one of the most common articles of clothes you'll find in dreams. Shoes in the dream realm represent preparation, calling, and destiny. If we think about shoes in the natural, shoes prepare and allow us to *walk* into something. Shoes can also be a play on words and may point to healing or the soul (heel=heal, sole=soul).

- **Many shoes**: many choices or many callings

- **Barefooted**: not prepared to walk into something
- **Tattered shoes**: a tough journey, hardships, trials, or poverty
- **Running shoes**: well equipped
- **Sandals**: humility, leisure, lackadaisical, not serious about where one is going
- **High heels**: something you think *highly* of or a lot of *healing* (heel)

Pants & Shirts

Pants and shirts represent covering. Usually, the color indicates the symbolism behind it.

- **Pants**: fulfilment of a calling, authority
- **Shorts**: a calling partially fulfilled, something "short" term

Bags & Purses

Bags and purses hold valuable things in them. In dreams, these things can represent something of monetary value or high value. Bags can also represent your heart since they hold "treasure" (Matthew 6:21).

If the contents of that bag were revealed, then that is where the meaning lies. For example, someone came to me with a dream, and in it, they were stopped by security because this person had a dangerous weapon in her purse. It was a black handgun, and this person had no idea how it had gotten there. The gun represented her speech and the situation that she was speaking against. She was unknowingly sabotaging a blessing by cursing it to herself. It goes to show that our words have a lot of weight.

Another possibility of interpretation is that bags can represent what you're carrying spiritually. A friend of mine shared a dream with me that she saw her brother carry a black backpack. It represented the burdens he was carrying that she was not keen to in the natural.

Jewelry

Jewelry usually holds high value and is priceless to the owner. In dreams, they can represent gifts of the Spirit, or just something priceless and valuable.

Food & Drink

So, food in dreams! Food in dreams can represent a myriad of different things, so it's not the easiest to sum it up in one category. If the dream is from God, food can represent information, ideas, or abstract concepts. If the source of the dream is demonic, then it could possibly be linked to witchcraft or demonic spirits.

Since my background is Nigerian-American (they believe *any* dreams that involve eating are demonic), I used to believe that whenever I ate or handled food in a dream, it was automatically a demonic attack and should be rebuked immediately upon waking. Well, I did that for some time, but I couldn't help but notice that the rest of the dream was highly symbolic, and I would discard the whole dream because of one triggering symbol. I became curious and began to decode highly symbolic dreams with me eating in it and became confused because the dream would be a God dream based on themes and context.

Don't get me wrong. If a dream is demonic and you are eating in it or someone is forcing you to eat something nasty, toxic, or spoiled, then it is definitely a demonic dream and probably tied to witchcraft. Those types of dreams should absolutely be rebuked, and you should go into warfare against it. The problem, though, is that we can't always assume every food or drink is demonic in a dream without context. I know it seems like a "better safe than sorry" method, but dreams are just not that simple. I understand that at the beginning of your journey in dream interpretation, you may want to cancel a dream quickly, but I'm suggesting that you not get comfortable in ignorance. Sit down with the dream and go through it and all its symbols. Make sure that you are not mistaking a God dream for a demonic dream.

Furthermore, it's important to note if the dream is highlighting a particular food or a meal in general. If you see something like a banquet with an assortment of food, then view the symbol as a collective rather than individually.

Also, don't forget about personal symbols. For example, if I saw myself preparing a vegan meal in a dream, I would understand it as beneficial because I see vegan food as a healthier option. Maybe another person thinks of bland or lacking something. Remember—don't overcomplicate symbols, check the context, and consider personal symbolism.

With all that being said, let's discuss some food and drink types and the possible symbolism behind it.

Food

- **Almonds**: anointing on a ministry (Num. 17:8)
- **Aloe**: Christ burial (Jn. 19:39)
- **Apple**: something forbidden or temptation (Gen. 3:6), wise words (Prov. 25:11), refreshing (Song. 2:5)

- **Bread**: life, communion (Matt. 26:26), covenant, multiplication, wisdom (Prov 9:2-5), essentials (Luke 11:3)
- **Butter**: something smooth, cunning (Ps 55:21)
- **Bubblegum**: a tricky situation that may be difficult to get out of
- **Cake**: celebration, milestone, achievement
- **Corn**: abundance, harvest
- **Crumbs**: something insignificant, a small amount to what is available
- **Eggs**: something new
- **Fish**: people (Matthew 4:19), multiplication (John 6:1-15), provision (John 21:6)
- **Fruit**: the result of something, fruit of someone's labor, something sweet (Song. 2:3)
- **Honey**: sweet, anointing, the Word of God and His Law (Ps. 19:7-10), prosperity (Ex 3:8)
  - **Honeycomb**: sweet words (Prov. 16:24)
- **Junk food**: something detrimental, harmful, gluttonous, quick and convenient
- **Lemons**: something sour, bitterness, a lesson, the hand you're dealt with (*when life gives you lemons, make lemonade*)
  - **Lemonade**: making the best out of a situation
- **Meat**: deeper revelation of the Word of God (1 Cor. 3:2)
- **Nuts**: delicacies (Gen 43:11)
- **Oil**: anointing (Ps. 23:5), Holy Spirit (Matt. 25:1-10)

- **Pomegranates**: ministry (Ex. 28:34)
- **Pork**: uncleanliness
- **Raisins**: something shriveled up, dying, decay, sweet
- **Ribs**: a wife or pertaining to marriage (Gen. 2:22)
- **Salt**: a believer's walk/character (Matt. 5:13), preservation/perseverance
- **Sweets**: something sweet, too much of a good thing, nonessentials, gossip (Prov. 18:8)
- **Vegetables/herbs/plants**: something beneficial, growth

Drinks

- **Coffee**: heightened level of activity, something needs to get moving, moving quickly or too quickly
- **Milk**: The Word of God (1 Pet 2:2), spiritual basics (1 Cor. 3:2), prosperity, abundance (Ex 3:8)
- **Water**: The Holy Spirit (if clear), replenishing
- **Wine**: communion, Jesus Christ, class, maturity
- **Liquor**: drunkenness, lack of control

Animals

Animals in dreams can represent spirits (good or bad), the dominant trait that is associated with it, or a biblical allegory. Keep in mind that animals can also be personal symbols depending on if you have the animal as a pet, work with animals, or have an affinity towards a certain type of animal.

Mammals

- **Bear**: judgement (2 Kings 2:24), strength, protective, territorial, anger
- **Bull**: a strong enemy (Ps. 22:12), clumsy (*bull* in a China store)
- **Camel**: long journey ahead, trails, endurance, perseverance, provision for journey
- **Cats**: independent, witchcraft (if black)
- **Cheetah**: fast, swift, play on words for "cheater"
- **Cow**: prosperity, wealth
- **Dogs**: loyalty, commitment, unbeliever (Matt 15:26)
    - **Pit bull**: higher ranking demonic spirit
- **Deer**: spiritual thirst (Ps. 42:1)
- **Donkey**: stubborn (Job 11:12), burdened
- **Elephant**: something that makes a big impact, something big that is ignored (the *elephant* in the room)
- **Fox**: sly, cunning (Lk.13:32)

- **Goat**: sinner, unbeliever (Matt. 25:33), stubborn, lack of discernment
- **Horse**: power, strength, war
  - **White horse**: salvation, rescue, redemption
  - **Black horse**: evil, warfare
  - **Red horse**: danger, opposition
- **Jackal**: scoffer, mocker (Ps. 44:19)
- **Lamb**: Jesus Christ (John 1:36), redemption
- **Leopard**: ambush, a sudden attack (Hos 13:7), swift
- **Lion**: Jesus Christ (Rev. 5:5), Satan (1 Pet. 5:8), territorial
- **Monkey**: childishness (*monkeying* around), something not taken seriously, mockery
- **Mouse/rat**: poverty, unclean, destruction
- **Pig**: unclean, ignorance, hypocrisy, gluttonous, ungrateful (Matt 7:6)
- **Rabbit**: multiplication, lust
- **Sheep**: follower, believer (Jn. 10:15), humility, stubborn, vulnerable
  - **Sheep's wool**: deception, fake, disguise, pretending to be something it's not
- **Wolf**: spiritual enemy (Matt. 10:16), something vicious (Ezek. 22:27)
- **Zebra**: ambiguous, lukewarm (black and white)

Sea Creatures

- **Alligator**: ancient spirit, generational
- **Fish**: people (Mark. 1:17)

- **Whale**: big impact in the Spirit, running away (book of Jonah), being redirected

Birds

- **Chicken**: fear, cowardly (don't be *chicken*), motherly (mother hen)
- **Dove**: Holy Spirit (Luke 3:22), peace, rest (Gen 8:11), easily deceived, senseless (Hosea 4:5)
- **Eagle**: prophetic ministry, prophet, swift and fast (2 Sam. 1:23)
- **Ostrich**: heartless (Lam. 4:3)
- **Owl**: wisdom
- **Raven**: messenger (Gen 8:7), provision (Luke 12:24)
- **Rooster**: an alarm, pride (Prov. 30:31)
- **Sparrow**: provision (Matt. 10:29)
- **Stork**: bringing something new, a blessing
- **Swan**: beauty for ashes, transformation
- **Vulture**: scavenger, greedy, decay, unclean, preying on weak

Reptiles/Amphibians

- **Dinosaur**: something ancient, old, the past, something that should be dead
- **Frogs**: lying, deceitful, unclean spirits/demons (Rev. 16:13-14)
- **Snake**: deception, hidden attack, lies (tails=tales), Satan

- White snake: false religion, occult
- Python: a spirit of divination (Acts 16:16)
- Cobra: a poisonous attack
- Rattlesnake: caution of an attack, a warning
- Turtle: slowness, delay, perseverance

Insects

- **Ants**: community, teamwork, perseverance, strength, industrious (Prov. 6:6), a nuisance
- **Bee**: painful attack, the enemy (Ps. 118:12) (Deut. 1:44)
- **Flies**: Beelzebub/Satan, occult, decay (Eccl. 10:1)
- **Honeybee**: sweetness, anointing
- **Leech**: greed (Prov. 30:15)
- **Locust**: the enemy (Jer. 51:14, Rev. 9:3), a curse (Ex. 10:1-20)
- **Roaches**: poverty
- **Scorpions**: demons (Lk. 10:19)
- **Snail**: slowness
- **Spider**: witchcraft, occult
  - **Spiderweb**: web of lies, trap
- **Wasp**: terror and confusion (Ex. 23:27-28), painful attack
- **Worm/Maggot**: devourer, destruction, curse, contempt (Ps. 22:6)

Communication

There are so many ways we communicate outside of verbally and nonverbally. As with any form of communication, most carry a specific message.

Phones

In the twenty-first century, phones are one of the most common ways we connect with one another. Whether ringing, texting, or calling, phones in dreams represent the transference of information or a message that is communicated. Phones can also represent something valuable that you carry.

- **Phone ringing**: an alert, a message attempt, something you should pay attention to
- **Lost phone**: lost mode of communication, lack of clarity or understanding
- **Exchanging numbers**: depending on who you are interacting with, that person or thing now has access to you
- **Text message**: a message

Computers

Computers contain information and are a way we communicate with each other as well. So with that being said, computers in dreams usually mean some type of information, or it is a literal symbol.

- **Computer crashing**: no access, inability to receive information, clarity, or insight
- **The internet**: the world, information
- **Viruses**: demonic attack

Emails

Emails carry a message, so pay attention to the contents of it in a dream or the circumstances surrounding it.

- **Failed email attempt**: unable to deliver a message, lack of clarity or understanding

Letters

Letters are becoming an old-school way of communication because of the time it takes to receive a letter. Letters in dreams can hold a general meaning of a message, or it can also mean a message that was slow to accept or understand.

Resources

Let's say you've read some things in this book that probably disturbed you. Perhaps you related to some things, and you're wondering how to overcome the power of the enemy. In this section, we will discuss some basic ways to engage in spiritual warfare and be delivered from evil spirits.

Spiritual Warfare & Deliverance

So what exactly is spiritual warfare? Simply put, it involves actively engaging and fighting back the enemy. Many modern-day churches shy away from this topic for many reasons. Perhaps some spiritual leaders are ignorant about how to engage, some may not think it's necessary, or some want their congregation to rely solely on them for spiritual support. Whatever the case is, it's extremely unfortunate that the body of Christ has been victims, in many cases, instead of victors.

People forget that Jesus Christ gave us his ministry mandate. Part of this mandate we have as disciples to cast out demons and heal the sick (Luke 9:1, Matt 10:1, Mark 16:17), and He told us that we have all authority to overcome the power of the enemy (Luke 10:19). What does this all mean? That means under the authority of Jesus Christ, we can continue His earthly ministry. Some ministries have audaciously boasted about that part of Jesus's ministry ceasing with the early Church. They believe that since the Church (worldwide) has been established, then there is no need for the gifts of the Spirit, exorcism/deliverance, and healing. This false doctrine has unknowingly kept many people who know that there is terribly something wrong in their lives bound. There are many people going through deep spiritual problems and the Church cannot help them. Lives are getting destroyed, but the Church watches defenseless.

Friends, you don't have to be a victim anymore. It's time to rise up and tap into the authority Christ has given us!

Without further ado, here are some strategies you can employ in the realm of prayer when you engage in spiritual warfare.

1. **Remember your identity**

As believers, we are co-heirs with Jesus Christ (Romans 8:17) and sons and daughters in God's Kingdom. One of the greatest lessons you must learn early in your walk is your *identity*. It's a very scary place to be when the enemy knows who you are, but you don't know who you are. In order to engage in any type of spiritual warfare, you have to be clear on your stance and your position in the Kingdom of God.

If you struggle with rejection or understanding your identity, you may want to meditate on the *Parable of the Prodigal Son* (Luke 15:11-32).

2. **Cover with the blood of Jesus**

The blood of Jesus washes away our sins (1 John 1:7), delivers us, and protects us (Colossians 1:13). Believing in the power of the blood and covering yourself with it through prayer is a great spiritual warfare tactic that you can use.

3. Put on full armor of God

The armor of God is mentioned in the Ephesians 6:10-18. This spiritual/symbolic armor has different parts that work together to protect us against the enemy. It may benefit you to meditate on those scriptures and to "pray them on" before engaging in spiritual warfare.

4. Repent

The Bible says that *all* have sinned and have fallen short of the glory of God (Romans 3:23) and if we say that we are without sin, then we are lying (1 John 1:8). That means that *everyone* on earth needs a Savior, and His name is Jesus Christ. We have to remember that sometimes we get attacked spiritually through our disobedience, which causes open doors (See Dreams from Demons). If you have sinned against God and man (which everybody has), then repent because His grace is sufficient for you (2 Corinthians 12:9). Name the things you have done to your Heavenly Father, and He will forgive you.

Also, repent from the sins of the generations before you. As we learned earlier in this book, generational curses are legal doors the enemy can go through until someone stops the cycle. Friend, be the curse breaker and repent on behalf of your forefathers' and ancestors' sins.

5. Renounce and command demons to go

Renouncing and commanding evil spirits to leave your life is one of the most important steps in spiritual warfare. Most people skip this part and keep looking to the Lord to do everything. Listen, if Jesus has given *us* the authority, He's not going to spoon feed us everything. As His disciples and beneficiaries to the new covenant, we can literally command the enemy to leave our lives in His name.

To renounce a sin, generational curse, or evil spirit, simply come out of agreement with it verbally. For example, you can say something like, "I come out of agreement with fear/lust/anger/etc. in Jesus name." or "I renounce the spirit of fear/lust/anger/etc. over my life in Jesus name." The exact words don't matter but the intentionality of the prayer does.

Next you must command those spirits to GO! Maybe you're wondering why they didn't leave simply at the repenting or renouncing. Well, you can see that action as the eviction notice. Just because you put an eviction notice on a house doesn't mean that whatever living there has left. The next thing to do is to bring the authorities and get them out. Commanding spirits to leave your life can be as simple as praying, "I command fear/lust/pride/etc. to leave my life and never return in Jesus name."

6. Pray and ask the Lord to lead you

So there are many ways to deal with different spirits and it takes the leading of the Lord to know exactly which route to take. Sometimes, you may need a mental renewal, other times you may simply need to follow the convictions the Lord has given you. In any case, you want to always rely on the Lord for wisdom and how to move in each situation.

7. Ask your spiritual leader

If you are a member of a local church or ministry, you may want to check with your spiritual covering on how to properly handle your individual situation. If it is a more serious case, they may be able to pray with you or direct you to someone who specializes in your particular case.

8. Seek out local ministries

Lastly, if you are not currently a member of a local church or your church does not specialize in your unique case, then you may want to seek other ministries. This takes prayer and the leading of the Holy Spirit. The Spirit of God may then lead you to a minister or ministry that can help you with your situation.

About the Author

Jumoke is a South Florida native and attended school at Florida International University in Miami, Florida. While pursuing a degree in computer engineering, she encountered Christ and gave her life to Him in November 2014.

While in college, she began to share her hair and faith journey on YouTube. Since 2012, her channel, *Jumoke*, has gained an audience of over 23,000 subscribers and over a million views. Jumoke speaks on a variety of topics including faith, prophetic words, natural hair care, singleness, dating, and of course, dream interpretation.

Throughout her natural hair journey, Jumoke was an advocate in helping women love and embrace their hair through her YouTube channel. She started a business called *Heritage Natural Hair Care* to meet the needs of women who struggle with their hair.

After she received her degree, the Lord began to prepare her for her callings. During her four years of singleness, Jumoke learned many things and received different revelations from the Lord about purposeful singleness. After some time, the Lord began to send different women her way and gave Jumoke the assignment to mentor them. Soon after in March 2020, she launched a ministry called *Single on Purpose International*. She now mentors over 140 women from all over the globe while developing her mentees as leaders.

While pioneering a new ministry, Jumoke noticed a problem within the realm of womanhood. She saw the art of femininity tainted by worldly sources and wanted to reintroduce femininity from a godly perspective. She launched a masterclass called *GodlyFem* in July 2020 to encourage women in their womanhood and to help heal those parts of them that hinders their wholeness.

Lastly, since Jumoke accepted salvation, she always had dreams but never knew what they meant. After years of studying under the Holy Spirit, she now teaches others about dream interpretation and helps people decode their dreams through virtual consultations and online courses.

Keep in touch with Jumoke:

- Website: https://jumokea.com/
- YouTube: https://www.youtube.com/c/Jumoke
- Instagram: @JumokeOfficial
- Twitter: @JumokeOfficial
- Facebook: https://www.facebook.com/JumokeOfficial

Learn more about dream interpretation:
https://CrackingTheDreamCode.com/
Instagram: @dreamcodebook

Join her ministry (women only), *Single on Purpose International*:
https://sop-int.com/

Check out her hair care line:
https://hnhaircare.com/

Learn more about godly femininity:
https://GodlyFem.com
Instagram: @GodlyFem

To give to Jumoke:
https://www.paypal.me/JumokeOfficial
CashApp: $JumokeAA

Printed in Great Britain
by Amazon